There is no more important assig[nment] [than the]
spiritual development of your ch[ildren.] [than]
Nothing. And *Glorious God, Glor[ious Gospel]* [will make]
this task a whole lot easier for a lot of moms and dads.

BOB LEPINE, *Co-Host, FamilyLife Today®*

Glorious God, Glorious Gospel is one of the most creative, practical,
and biblically-faithful overviews of central aspects of Gospel truth
available for parents to use with their children. I can only imagine
the hours of joyful learning and sharing that will take place in
homes where these lessons are studied together. What a wonderful
tool for families, and for the next generations of Christians who
know the Gospel and know their gracious and glorious God well.

BRUCE WARE, *Ph.D., Professor of Christian Theology, The Southern
Baptist Theological Seminary and author of* Big Truths for Young Hearts

We know how loud and unavoidable the voice of the world is that
speaks into the lives of our children, and we long for God's voice to be
heard in their lives. *Glorious God, Glorious Gospel* provides everything
parents need for meaningful, interactive discussions about foundational
truths and essential equipping for every parent who is intimidated
by the idea of leading family times focused on biblical truth.

NANCY GUTHRIE, *author of* One Year of Dinner
Table Devotions & Discussion-Starters

Sally Michael and Jill Nelson have captured the essence of their entire
Sunday school curriculum in one easy-to-use family devotional. Use
Glorious God, Glorious Gospel with your family and take your children
through a heart-engaging study of our awesome God and His merciful
Gospel rescue. You'll be so glad you did, and so will your kids.

MARTY MACHOWSKI, *pastor and author of* The Ology,
The Gospel Story Bible, *and* Dragon Seed

All parents want to pass on Gospel truths to our children but we
sometimes feel inadequate or inconsistent. *Glorious God, Glorious
Gospel* helps fathers and mothers introduce the deep and delightful
truths of Scripture to our children, skillfully targeting their hearts,
minds, and wills. The layout is easy to read, the structure is flexible
for different family schedules, and the supplemental materials aid
application. This book is an incredibly valuable tool for parents who want
to guide their family through God's wise and wonderful plan of salvation.

NICOLE WHITACRE, *author of* True Feelings, True Beauty, *and*
Girl Talk: Mother-Daughter Conversations on Biblical Womanhood

One of the most pressing needs when it comes to training parents to disciple their children is simple, interactive, Gospel-centered family devotional curriculum. *Glorious God, Glorious Gospel* fills that gap admirably.

TIMOTHY PAUL JONES, *Ph.D., Professor of Christian Family Ministry, The Southern Baptist Theological Seminary and author of* Family Ministry Field Guide

Children are gifts from God and are examples of His amazing grace and generosity. Parenting those children is rewarding, but it is also intimidating. We are to faithfully raise them in the discipline and instruction of God's Word. That is a daunting task. And resources like *Glorious God, Glorious Gospel* help make that task less intimidating. Sally Michael and Jill Nelson have produced a remarkable devotional that will help us glorify God through the faithful, systematic, and thorough teaching of God's glorious Gospel to our children, that they might live as faithful disciples for the glory of God.

ANDREW ROGERS, *Ph.D., Professor of Biblical Counseling, Boyce College*

In *Glorious God, Glorious Gospel* you will find superb interactive material which expresses the riches of the Bible in child-appropriate language and ideas with plenty to engage their young hearts and minds. But this is more than just another resource for family devotions.

Consider these words: 'Solid theology. Rich spiritual food.' Not usually associated with family devotions material *Glorious God, Glorious Gospel* is full of these things. It will enable parents to fulfill their calling to raise their children to know and love God in Christ deeply.

What about these words: 'God-centered, Christ-exalting, Bible-saturated'? *Glorious God, Glorious Gospel* contains the biblical themes emphasized in the ministry of John Piper. It will enable families to aim high in what they communicate to and desire for their children.

IAN FRY, *Associate Minister for Families, St. Ebbe's Church, Oxford, England*

Glorious God, Glorious Gospel is a great new tool to help you disciple your children. These are deep, biblical truths about God and the Gospel. Nothing fluffy or fuzzy, here. And while it's filled with questions to spark conversation and increase understanding, the real goal is to engage your kid's hearts. Reading these devotions, I found myself regularly responding, "Yes, that's true! God really is glorious!" That's how we pray our children will respond, by God's grace, with loving hearts and joyful obedience.

BRUCE HOFFMIRE, *Pastor of Children's Ministries, CrossWay Community Church, Bristol, Wis.*

Glorious GOD
Glorious GOSPEL

AN INTERACTIVE
FAMILY DEVOTIONAL

SALLY MICHAEL & JILL NELSON

Truth:78 / Equipping the Next Generations
to Know, Honor, and Treasure God

PRODUCTION TEAM

AUTHORS
Sally Michael
Jill Nelson

PROJECT DIRECTOR
Brian Eaton

PROJECT MANAGERS
Karen Hieb
Steve Watters

THEOLOGICAL EDITOR
Gary Steward

PROJECT SUPPORT
Lori Myers
Suzy Plocher
Lis Trouten
Holly Urbanski

ILLUSTRATOR
Nicole Manuel

DESIGNER
Rachel Golias

Glorious God, Glorious Gospel

© 2018 by Next Generation Resources, Inc. and Jill Nelson. Illustrations by Truth78.

All rights reserved. No part of this publication may be reproduced in any form without written permission from Truth78.

Published in Minneapolis, Minnesota by Truth78.

All Scripture quotations, unless otherwise noted, are from the ESV® Bible (The Holy Bible, English Standard Version®) copyright © 2001 by Crossway, a publishing ministry of Good News Publishers. Used by permission. All rights reserved. ESV Text Edition: 2016.

Photographs © iStock.

ISBN-13: 978-0-9969869-3-9

Truth:78 / Equipping the Next Generations to Know, Honor, and Treasure God

Truth78.org · info@Truth78.org · 877.400.1414 · @Truth78org

For our grandchildren,
Anna, Katie, Joshua, David,
Elizabeth, Ellie, Nate, and Ronan

By God's grace, may you grow up
to be men and women who know,
honor, and treasure God,
setting your hope in Christ alone,
so that you will live as faithful
disciples for the glory of God!

*I give thanks to you,
O Lord my God,
with my whole heart,
and I will glorify
your name forever.*

PSALM 86:12

CONTENTS

PREFACE

As parents, we want many things to be true of our children as they grow and mature. For example, we want our children to be loving, respectful, caring, productive, motivated, resilient, happy, and more. All are good things and worthwhile goals. All require some measure of our time and attention as we instruct and train our children toward these goals. But consider these words from 3 John 1:4:

> *I have no greater joy than to hear that*
> *my children are walking in the truth.*

This simple statement can serve to orient all of our parenting. It directs us to what is most important: More than anything else, our children need to know, embrace, and walk in the truth—the truth of God. The truth revealed in His Word has the power to make them wise for salvation through faith in Jesus Christ—the truth that all-satisfying and everlasting joy is found in Him alone, the truth that saving faith will be evidenced by a life that submits to the Savior and walks in His ways.

What a wonderful privilege and sacred responsibility God has entrusted to us! It aims and steers our parenting toward one grand vision for our children, which is reflected in Truth78's Vision Statement:

> **Our vision is that the next generations know,**
> **honor, and treasure God, setting their hope**
> **in Christ alone, so that they will live as**
> **faithful disciples for the glory of God.**

This resource has been developed to help parents in this grand endeavor. This tool is meant to be a small part of a lifetime of teaching, training, and discipling children in the Word of God.

> **At its very heart, *Glorious God, Glorious Gospel* is meant to clearly and succinctly summarize the essence, means, and goal of the Gospel.**

We hope and pray that you find it a valuable tool that serves your family as you explore together the majestic truth of our glorious God and His glorious Gospel!

INTRODUCTION

If we, as parents, are to pursue a God-glorifying vision for our children, we must make sure to carefully prioritize and maximize our children's spiritual instruction. While there is an important and God-ordained role for the wider body of Christ (the church) in biblical instruction, parents have the primary responsibility and the greatest opportunity to influence their children's spiritual development. (See Deuteronomy 6:4-9.)

One thing that often hinders parents in this regard is the pressure of competing demands on our time and energy. These are valid concerns. But consider for a moment these thoughts from Pastor Chap Bettis:

> "Where does discipling my child fit with the other priorities?" Surrounding us are parents making superhuman sacrifices for their children's soccer practice, hockey practice (5 a.m. ice time?), academic progress, and music lessons (two instruments at the same time?). We can be tempted to follow them. While we may give lip service to discipling our children, the reality comes when we start prioritizing activities.
>
> The apostle John expressed his heart for his spiritual children when he wrote, "I have no greater joy than to hear that my children are walking in the truth" (3 John 4). Here lies the crux of the matter: The first battleground of family discipleship is not my child's heart—it is my heart. Each parent must

> decide whether he is more concerned that his child
> be accepted into Heaven, or "Harvard." We all have
> "Harvards"—those worldly successes we desire for
> our children, but the question remains, "Which is
> most important to me?" Each parent must finish
> the sentence "I have no greater joy than..."
>
> I would emphasize here that the challenge of priorities
> is often not the good versus the bad, rather, the
> good versus the better. Given a finite amount of
> time, energy, and money, what will you choose?[1]

As parents, our first priority must be our desire for our children's spiritual development. Then we can order our time and energies accordingly. One way to do this is to establish a regular time of formal biblical instruction in the home through family devotions.

ABOUT THIS DEVOTIONAL RESOURCE

This resource has been developed as a family devotional for parents to use with their children to ground them in the essential, foundational, and glorious truths of the Gospel. These truths take into account the whole counsel of God by answering important questions, such as:

> Who is God, and what is He like?
>
> Why do I exist? How am I to act toward God?
>
> What is my greatest problem and need?
>
> What has God done to solve this problem?
>
> How can I be saved?
>
> How should I now live?

Too often children are given mere bits and pieces of Gospel truth apart from the wider and deeper context of these truths. To repeatedly say, "Jesus died to save us from our sins," is absolutely true, but this statement alone does not provide the amazing foundation on which

[1]Bettis, Chap. *The Disciple-Making Parent: A Comprehensive Guidebook for Raising Your Children to Love and Follow Jesus Christ.* (Cumberland, Rhode Island: Diamond Hill Publishing, 2016), 17.

this truth is built. And without that foundation, the enormous personal implications this truth demands are minimized.

Therefore, there is an intentional flow to the 15 chapters. Each chapter builds on the previous one, providing a logical flow of thought. It is important to note that the first eight chapters focus mainly on Old Testament texts, as these provide the progressive unfolding of God's redemptive plan, which is crucial for understanding the Person and work of Christ. After completing all 15 chapters, you will have presented your children with a clear, succinct summary of the Gospel. But keep in mind that this study is by no means exhaustive in its breadth or depth!

INTERACTIVE DEVOTIONAL

The word "interactive" has been included in the subtitle of this resource for a very good reason. We want your children to be encouraged to participate with the material. Mainly this will consist of asking questions at key points, especially questions specifically related to biblical texts. This will help your children remain more focused, attentive, and interested in the material. This method also helps foster important critical thinking and serves to help parents discern their child's biblical knowledge and spiritual maturity.

UNDERSTANDING THE DEVOTIONAL'S TEACHING PHILOSOPHY AND METHODOLOGY

We believe that there is an important progression involved in encouraging our children for a life of faith in Christ. To put it very succinctly: MIND → HEART → WILL. Children must first be presented with biblical truth for their minds to absorb, ponder, and understand. Knowledge of God and His Word is the essential first step for faith (Romans 10:17). You cannot trust, love, and act upon what you do not know. Next, that truth must go beyond mere knowledge. It must reach and transform the heart so that children might truly embrace, cherish, and love the truth—specifically love of God through faith in Christ. Finally, this love will affect the will as it comes under submission to Christ, producing decisions, choices, words, and actions that are pleasing to God.

While we must fully acknowledge that only God can bring about this Spirit-wrought, grace-dependent transformation, we believe that it is our responsibility to guide, inspire, and implore our children to make a personal and sincere response to God's truth in their minds, hearts, and will. Therefore, each chapter includes three major, distinct sections to encourage this:

Instruct the Mind

Engage the Heart

Influence the Will

HOW TO USE
THE MATERIAL

Within each chapter, text in **bold** indicates a question. Suggested or anticipated answers to some questions are provided in [brackets]. Text in (parentheses) may be instructions for you or simpler terminology for younger children.

Each chapter is divided into the following seven parts:

TITLE

Signifies the main idea presented.

INTRODUCTION FOR PARENTS

To be read by parents beforehand for their own spiritual benefit and preparation.

PIQUE THEIR INTEREST

A brief "hook" to grab your children's attention and direct their thinking toward the subject matter of the chapter.

INSTRUCT THE MIND

This is the actual material that will be read to your family. Depending upon the age of your children and the depth of discussion you encourage at various points, this section can take anywhere from five to 10 minutes. The goal during this time is to present biblical truth for the mind to absorb. To help with this vital process, questions are provided to help children rightly interpret and understand key texts and other biblical truths. Some questions are meant to spur further reflection, recall previous truths learned, and propose personal application. And some questions are provided so that younger children can participate. If you have older children, you may just want to state the truth implied in these simpler questions. Other easy-to-answer questions, though, are intended to encourage children to observe the text, a primary step toward developing Bible study skills. When your child reads the Bible, encourage him to not simply read the text, but to make observations that lead to greater understanding of the text.

PLEASE NOTE: Unless you plan to extend this time significantly, do not require your children to look up the Bible texts.

ENGAGE THE HEART

The Engage the Heart section is meant to be conversational, engaging your child's heart, and it has a three-fold purpose:

- to cause your family to interact with spiritual truth in such a way that it does not merely land on the intellect, but encourages your heart to be drawn to the truth.

- to help you and your child to identify how the truth applies practically to everyday life.

- to aid parents in understanding how to engage their children in spiritual discussions.

Because the Holy Spirit will be at work in different ways in the hearts of different children, the Engage the Heart questions are simply *suggestions* of some of the possible discussion directions you can explore. You will not be able to explore all the possible conversations, or to cause your child's heart to soften toward God. Therefore, it is imperative that you pray for the Lord to guide you as you begin to engage your child in conversation. Feel free to deviate from the noted questions and follow up on children's comments.

INFLUENCE THE WILL

When our children's hearts are inclined to love the Lord and trust His Word, they will desire to walk in His ways, responding in obedience to His commands. For this reason, you will want to note if your child is going beyond understanding how the truth intersects with daily life to actually following the truth, being a doer of the Word. Does your child want to follow Jesus and walk in all His ways? Helping your child to decide on a concrete step he can take will give him a specific means of obeying God. It will take the theoretical and make it practical and applicable for him.

FAMILY WORSHIP TIME

If your family has time and you are so inclined, this section provides a hymn for the family to study and then sing together. Why hymns? Here are a few reasons:

- Hymns are a wonderful means of memorizing important biblical truths. Even before a child can understand the words and meaning, they can memorize the words and tunes—and usually enjoy doing so.

- Hymns provide a wonderful means of encouraging a right heart response to God. The Bible is filled with songs of praise to God. It is a means of grace, and music is a natural way to express deep, heartfelt emotions.

- Singing praise to God together as a family is a way to grow in your love for God and your love for one another. Something very important is "caught" by your children when they observe you in heartfelt praise to God. It makes a lasting impression on them.

All hymns in this interactive devotional include a reference to a book titled, *Hymns of Grace* (published by The Master's Seminary Press, hymnsofgrace.com). We highly recommend this hymnal for your family.

It is modestly priced, and the publisher has carefully chosen the hymns based on their theological content. For those who do not choose to purchase a hymnal, these hymns are easy to find on the internet.

ADAPTING THE MATERIAL TO YOUR DESIRED FREQUENCY AND TIME FRAME

The material is very flexible. You can decide on the time frame that works best for your family and make the necessary adjustments. For example, you could do 10 minutes a day every day, or 30 minutes one day a week. Here are some general ways you could use the material:

- A DAILY DEVOTIONAL: Cover one chapter every day, five days a week, for a total of three weeks.

- A WEEKLY DEVOTIONAL: Cover one entire chapter, once a week, for 15 weeks; or parts of one chapter throughout the week, doing whatever sections at whatever intervals you choose.

- AN EXTENDED DAILY DEVOTIONAL: Cover one chapter every week, but break each chapter into daily sections. For example, do "Instruct the Mind" on Monday, do various "Engage the Heart" discussions on Tuesday through Thursday, and do the "Family Worship Time" on Friday.

- A DEVOTIONAL TO USE DURING A ONCE-A-WEEK EXTENDED FAMILY NIGHT: a time for study and special family activity, and fun.

- YOUR FAMILY PACE: Cover as much or as little as you wish in whatever time frame works for your family.

OPTIONAL RESOURCES

In order to enhance your child's experience there are two optional resources you may wish to purchase from Truth78:

- *Glorious God, Glorious Gospel Notebook* (for elementary age children)
- *Glorious God, Glorious Gospel Coloring Book* (for younger children)

TIPS FOR
LEADING
FAMILY DEVOTIONS

For some, especially those who grew up in the absence of family devotion time, leading family devotions can feel intimidating and stressful. We hope that this resource will provide you with an easy-to-use tool that will give you a measure of confidence and joy. But there are also a variety of things that you can do to create a more conducive environment for your family.

1. Have a regularly scheduled (and child friendly) time for devotions.

2. Keep track of time—stretch your child's attention span, but don't exasperate them.

3. It is preferred that (if possible) the father should lead the devotional time.

4. Choose a regular place in your home—one with as few distractions as possible (no TV, etc.).

5. Begin your time with prayer.

6. Put any and all electronic devices (e.g. phones, tablets) out of reach.

7. End in prayer.

8. In order to motivate a younger child's attentiveness, consider following your devotional time with a special snack or dessert.

Know

Honor

Treasure

When God speaks through the Bible, **THINGS HAPPEN.**

KNOWING GOD'S WORD

INTRODUCTION FOR PARENTS

President Theodore Roosevelt once said:

> **A thorough knowledge of the Bible**
> **is more important than a college education.**

Whatever Roosevelt's intention in saying this, his statement is true. It is true because the sovereign God of the universe has revealed Himself in a Book that can be read, studied, and understood. That, in and of itself, is a glorious reality. Furthermore, it is through this Book—the Scriptures—that we learn the most important truths ever given to man, truths that are essential for our lasting joy. The Bible acquaints us with God's divine character, His glorious works and deeds, and His redemptive purposes accomplished through Christ on behalf of His chosen people.

There is a popular trend, especially seen in children's Bible materials, that highlights these truths by conveying that the Bible is, first and foremost, a *story*. Yes, in one sense, the Bible is one grand story, and our children need to know the metanarrative of Scripture that unifies and clarifies all the diverse books, genres, and themes. However, the Bible is also much more than a story! It is the God-breathed, authoritative Word of God. God has given it innate power. It is crucial that we teach our children this greater understanding of the Bible so that they might be encouraged to truly know, love, and trust the Author of the Bible and joyfully submit their lives to Him.

01

GATHER: Bible, tissue or piece of paper

PIQUE THEIR INTEREST

Ask each member of the family to name a favorite book and then briefly describe a favorite character, event, or some other quality he or she likes about the book.

> There are many wonderful books. Some are silly stories that make us laugh. Some may be sad in parts but have a "happily ever after" ending. These are often "pretend" stories. But some books tell true stories of exciting adventures that make us want to join in, or that tell us about someone who has done something wonderful. Other books teach us important things we need to know. No matter how old or young you are, books are really special.
>
> But there is one book that stands apart from all others. **What is this book?** (Hold up a BIBLE.)

❓ **Why does the Bible stand apart from all other books? Why is it so special?** (Encourage a few brief responses.)

INSTRUCT THE MIND

Read and interact with the following Scriptures.

All Scripture is breathed out by God...
—2 TIMOTHY 3:16A

ILLUSTRATE: Have your child hold a PIECE OF PAPER or TISSUE in front of his face and instruct him to blow on the paper or tissue like he is blowing out a candle. **Where did the air that moved the paper or tissue come from?** [inside of your child]

❓ **Where did the words of the Bible—all Scripture—come from?** [God. It was as if God "breathed them out."] **So, even though God**

4

01

used men to write the words we see in the Bible, who is actually speaking to us when we read the Bible? [God]

Every word of God proves true;—PROVERBS 30:5A

...your word is truth.—JOHN 17:17B

Is some of the Bible true? Is most of it true? What do these two verses tell us? [Every word proves true. The entire Bible is truth.] So when the Bible says something about what God is like or how we are to act toward Him, does it have the "final say"? Should we believe what God has said?

Forever, O LORD, your word is firmly fixed
in the heavens.—PSALM 119:89

ILLUSTRATE: What would make a better road to drive on? Cement or ice? What will happen to the ice on a warm sunny day? How can this example help us to understand this verse?

Will the words of the Bible ever change and become unreliable? Will God change His mind and decide to tell us something different from what He has told us in the Bible? What three words does this verse use to tell us that God's Word will not change? [forever, firmly, fixed] Can you think of one example in which people are now trying to say that God's Word is no longer relevant or true?

> God's Word is able to revive the soul, make wise the simple, rejoice the heart, and enlighten the eyes.

The law of the LORD is perfect, reviving the soul;
the testimony of the LORD is sure, making wise
*the simple; *8*the precepts of the LORD are right,*
rejoicing the heart; the commandment of the LORD
is pure, enlightening the eyes;—PSALM 19:7-8

In these verses, what do the words "law," "testimony," "precepts," and "commandments" have in common? [They are all "of the LORD"—God. They are all part of the Bible.]

01

According to these verses, **what four things is God's Word able to do in our lives?** [revive the soul, make wise the simple, rejoice the heart, and enlighten the eyes] **Why is God's Word able to do these kinds of things?** [It is perfect, sure, right, and pure. It's powerful, and is from God Himself. It is "living and active." (See Hebrews 4:12.)]

Suppose someone said, "All that's very nice, but I really don't need the Bible." **What would you say to him?** (Encourage some brief responses and then read the text below.)

> *...from childhood you have been acquainted*
> *with the sacred writings, which are able*
> *to make you wise for salvation through*
> *faith in Christ Jesus.*—2 TIMOTHY 3:15

Why must you know the Bible? [It's able to make a person wise for salvation through faith in Christ.]

SUMMARY

The Bible is like no other book. Yes, in some ways the Bible is a type of story—"the best, true story ever written." But the Bible is much more than a story. The Bible is the one true God telling us the most important things we need to know. We need to know who He is, what He is like, and how we are to act toward Him. When God

> **Through the Bible, God tells us about our greatest need and problem, and God's perfect provision and solution. The Bible tells us the only way to have lasting joy and happiness.**

tells us something in the Bible, that is the way it is. God has the final say. There is no higher authority. When God speaks through the Bible, things happen. The Bible is powerful and active. When God speaks through the Bible, everyone must listen—both children and adults, people in our neighborhood, and people all around the world. Through the Bible, God tells us about our greatest need and problem, and God's perfect provision and solution. The Bible tells us the only way to have lasting joy and happiness.

No other book is more important than the Bible. It is "one of a kind" and perfect in every way. It is God's Holy Word.

01

ENGAGE THE HEART

Choose one or more of the following topics to discuss. You may need to simplify the language or concepts for younger children. Suggestions for wording changes and questions specifically geared toward younger children are provided in parentheses.

GOD-BREATHED SCRIPTURE

There are more than 31,000 verses in the Bible...all of them coming from God Himself. **What does this tell you about God?**

Point your child to the vastness of God's wisdom and knowledge, the protection of God over His Word, which was produced by 44 human authors over a period of about 1,500 years, and God's desire to communicate with man.

Why is it so important to God to preserve a written record of His commands and deeds? The Bible is a great gift to us. How is God's grace and kindness shown in giving us the Bible? How can you tell if you treasure the Bible?

(What would happen if God's Word was not written and we only heard it from what people have remembered about it? What does having a written Word of God show you about the wisdom and goodness of God?)

EVERY WORD TRUE

Why is truth more important than opinion? What verses or parts of the Bible are easy for you to trust? What verses or parts are harder for you to trust? Why? How can you measure how much you trust in the truthfulness of God's Word?

01

(Suppose you read a verse in the Bible that tells you something you must do—like obey your parents, as it says in Ephesians 6:1. Would it be okay for you to say, "I don't really have to do what it says"? Why not?)

FOREVER FIXED

> *Every word of God proves true;*
>
> PROVERBS 30:5A

Why is it important that God's Word is "forever fixed" or permanent? What are some things in your life that might change? How does that affect you? What is most troubling or worrisome? What things will not change? What is most comforting about this? What can you be confident or sure of? Is there a verse you can stand on for reassurance, peace, and stability (comfort, peace, encouragement, and strength)? What about this verse gives you confidence for the future?

Why would it be inadequate (not enough, not complete) to say that the Bible is mostly a story? Why is it so important that the Bible is more than a story? What "more" is it? Why is this so important? How does this affect your life?

(The word "authoritative" means that it can be trusted as being correct and true. What does it mean that the Bible is the authoritative Word of God?[1] If the Bible was only a story and not God's authoritative Word, what would that mean?)

THE BLESSING OF GOD'S LAW

The words "law," "testimony," "precepts," and "commandments" in Psalm 19 mean God's whole mind and will—everything that God wants us to believe and do. It is God's whole teaching on what we should think and how we should act.

Explain how the words "perfect," "sure," "right," and "pure" rightly characterize or describe God's Word.

---

[1] Make sure that your child understands not only that it is correct and true, but also it carries the weight of demanding obedience.

01

How does the Bible—the wisdom and will of God—revive the soul? How does it make the simple wise? How does it cause the heart to rejoice? How does it enlighten the eyes?

Make sure your child understands that when the Bible "enlightens the eyes," it opens our eyes to our sinfulness, the holy and righteous nature of God, our need for a Savior or sin-bearer, and what it means to be a disciple of Jesus.

Explain one way that the Bible has refreshed you or given you hope, one way it has given you wisdom by showing you the right thing to think or do, one way it has caused you to rejoice, and one way that it has opened your eyes to the character of God and your true condition.

Are there any verses that you can share that have been especially encouraging, helpful, comforting, or convicting to you? What is it about these verses that has touched your heart?

SALVATION

Knowing the Bible is not the same as knowing or having a relationship with God. How is the Bible "able to make you wise for salvation"? How can we obtain salvation?

Make sure your child knows that faith in Jesus is more than just believing that He came to earth, died on the cross, and rose again. Help your child understand what it means to place your confidence in Jesus, trusting in Him alone for salvation, and entrusting your future to Him so as to embrace His lordship.

How can we pray for you?

INFLUENCE THE
WILL

What action or actions can you take this week to strengthen your determination to read the Word, memorize the Word, or trust the Word?

01 # FAMILY WORSHIP TIME

Read the words of the hymn "Speak, O Lord" by Keith Getty and Stuart Townend (*Hymns of Grace*, 368, or you can find it on the internet). As you read the words, have your children raise their hands or speak up when they hear God's Word being described in a special way. Read the hymn again, and this time ask the children to identify words that tell how we are to respond to God's Word. Sing the hymn together.

PRAYER TIME

How can you pray for your children and their salvation?

OUR FAMILY VERSES

Think through different situations and what you feel—joyful, sad, thankful, scared, etc. Write down a family verse to recite during each of those times.

Situation or feeling:	A verse to encourage our family:

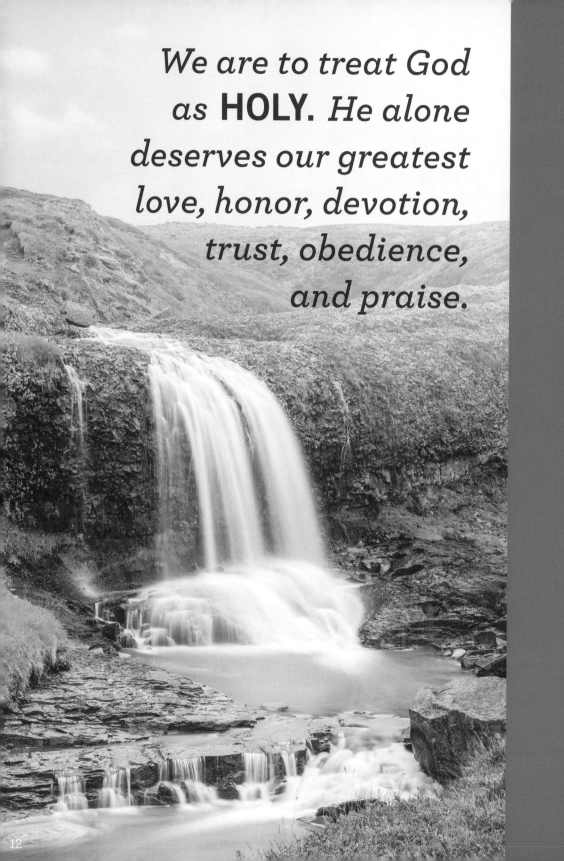

We are to treat God as **HOLY.** *He alone deserves our greatest love, honor, devotion, trust, obedience, and praise.*

KNOWING GOD'S DIVINE CHARACTER

INTRODUCTION FOR PARENTS

In his classic work, *The Knowledge of the Holy*, A.W. Tozer writes:

> The heaviest obligation lying upon the Christian Church today is to purify and elevate her concept of God until it is once more worthy of Him—and of her...We do the greatest service to the next generation of Christians by passing on to them undimmed and undiminished that noble concept of God which we received from our Hebrew and Christian fathers of generations past. [1]

So, we must ask the question: Are we falling short of this obligation? Could it be that, in our heartfelt desire to see our children come to salvation in Jesus, we minimize the majestic revelation of God's character as taught in the Old Testament? Are we quick to emphasize the Person and work of Jesus, while neglecting a robust understanding of the divine character of the *LORD* God? As Paul reminded Timothy, the sacred Scriptures—which include the whole Old Testament—are meant to make us wise for salvation in Christ (2 Timothy 3:15). When we see who God is and what He is like, we are given the proper context in which to understand the necessity, essence, means, and goal of salvation.

[1] Tozer, A.W. *The Knowledge of the Holy: The Attributes of God: Their Meaning in the Christian Life.* (New York, N.Y.: HarperCollins Publishers, 1961), 4.

Consider the words of the great Presbyterian theologian J. Gresham Machen:

02

> **...when men say that we know God only as He is revealed in Jesus, they are denying all real knowledge of God whatever. For unless there be some idea of God independent of Jesus, the ascription of deity to Jesus has no meaning. To say, "Jesus is God," is meaningless unless the word "God" has an antecedent meaning attached to it...[2]**

In today's devotion, we will explore some essential "antecedents" of God's character as revealed in the Old Testament. While the list is not exhaustive, it is meant to help your child understand God's divine character and serve his or her understanding of salvation.

> **GATHER:** Two pieces of paper, pen or pencil

PIQUE THEIR INTEREST

At the top of a PIECE OF PAPER, write the name of a famous person or extended family member with whom your child is familiar. Explain that you are going to give everyone 60 seconds to call out as many words or phrases as possible that describe this person. Designate someone to write these descriptive words or phrases on the paper.

If you met someone who didn't know this person, would the words we wrote help that person to know _(name of the person you've been describing)_? Do you think after describing who _(this person)_ is and what _(he or she)_ is like, someone would say "Wow, _(he or she)_ sounds great! I wish I could meet _(him or her)_"? Why or why not?

Summarize the purpose of this activity with the following points.

....
[2] Machen, J. Gresham. *Christianity and Liberalism*. (Grand Rapids, Mich.: Wm. B. Eerdmans Publishing Co., New Edition, 2009), 48-49.

- The words used to describe who a person is and what he or she is like are important.
- These words reflect a person's character.
- These words can serve to bring about admiration, respect, trust, love, etc. for that person.

02

INSTRUCT THE
MIND

On the top of another PIECE OF PAPER write "YHWH → the LORD God." Quickly explain that the one true God also has a special personal name. He first revealed this special name to Moses and the people of Israel. In the language of the Old Testament (Hebrew), it was written with the letters "YHWH." It is used more than 6,800 times in the Old Testament. Many people pronounce it as "Yahweh," and it is often seen (translated) in Bibles as "the LORD." It is a name that belongs to God alone.

❓ Are there words and phrases that describe what the LORD is like? Can you give any examples? Where did you get these from?

Read the following Scriptures and ask those listening to identify key words that describe the LORD God. Quickly write these on the paper. There are examples provided in [brackets].

> *The Rock, his work is perfect, for all his ways are justice. A God of faithfulness and without iniquity, just and upright is he.*—DEUTERONOMY 32:4

[perfect, faithful, just, without sin]

> *Oh, taste and see that the LORD is good!*
> —PSALM 34:8A

[good]

> *But you, O Lord, are a God merciful and gracious, slow to anger and abounding in steadfast love and faithfulness.*—PSALM 86:15

[merciful, gracious, slow to anger (or patient), loving, faithful]

He who dwells in the shelter of the Most High will abide in the shadow of the Almighty.—PSALM 91:1

[Most High, Almighty (all-powerful)]

02

Righteous are you, O LORD, and right are your rules.
—PSALM 119:137

[righteous]

*Have you not known? Have you not heard?
The LORD is the everlasting God, the Creator of the
ends of the earth. He does not faint or grow weary;
his understanding is unsearchable.*—ISAIAH 40:28

[everlasting (or eternal), never-tiring, all-knowing]

"I, I am the LORD, and besides me there is no savior."
—ISAIAH 43:11

[the only Savior]

*But the LORD is the true God; he is the living God
and the everlasting King.*—JEREMIAH 10:10a

[true God, living, King]

*"Can a man hide himself in secret places
so that I cannot see him? declares the LORD.
Do I not fill heaven and earth? declares the LORD."*
—JEREMIAH 23:24

[everywhere all the time (or omnipresent)]

"For I the LORD do not change;"—MALACHI 3:6a

[unchanging]

*"(for you shall worship no other god, for the LORD,
whose name is Jealous, is a jealous God),"*
—EXODUS 34:14

[jealous, God alone deserves worship]

> ..."The hand of our God is for good on all
> who seek him, and the power of his wrath is
> against all who forsake him."—EZRA 8:22B

[good, wrathful (rightful anger)]

02

❓ **Based on these verses, would you say the LORD God is similar or comparable to other famous people? Why not? How is the LORD God completely "set apart" from anyone or anything else? Because these things are true of God, how does He deserve to be treated?** (Encourage some thoughtful responses.)

Read the following passage:

> There is none like you among the gods, O Lord, nor are there any works like yours. ⁹ All the nations you have made shall come and worship before you, O Lord, and shall glorify your name. ¹⁰ For you are great and do wondrous things; you alone are God. ¹¹ Teach me your way, O LORD, that I may walk in your truth; unite my heart to fear your name. ¹² I give thanks to you, O Lord my God, with my whole heart, and I will glorify your name forever.—PSALM 86:8-12

SUMMARY

The LORD God is unlike anyone or anything else. The LORD God has no equal. His greatness and worth is infinite, meaning it goes beyond anything we can think or imagine. God is "one of a kind." That is why God calls Himself "the Holy One."

God wants us to know about Him. That is why He gave us His Word, the Bible. As you read the Bible, every word on every page is telling you something important that you need to know about the holy God. Every time you read a verse or story from the Bible, the first question you should ask is, "What does this tell me about who God is and what He is like?" In response, we are to treat God as Holy. He alone deserves our greatest love, honor, devotion, trust, obedience, and praise.

> As you read the Bible, every word on every page is telling you something important that you need to know about the holy God.

ENGAGE THE HEART

02

Choose one or more of the following topics to discuss.

WHAT IS GOD LIKE?

The verses we read give us a long list of words that describe what God is like: perfect, faithful, just, sinless, good, merciful, gracious, slow to anger (patient), loving, faithful, all-powerful, righteous, eternal (everlasting), never-tiring, all-knowing, omnipresent (everywhere all the time), unchanging. Discuss some of these characteristics by answering the following questions together:

What does it mean that God is _____(characteristic)_____?

What are some examples of God's _____(characteristic)_____?

Use your imagination and describe what it would be like if God were not _____(characteristic)_____.

How does imagining God being the opposite of what He really is, affect your heart toward Him?

God is also the only Savior, the true and living God, and the King. **Why are these characteristics so important? What would it mean if these characteristics were not true of God? How can knowing these characteristics give you great peace, encouragement, confidence, and joy?**

When the Bible talks about God being "jealous" it means that He "does not share His glory or the honor and praise He deserves." **Why is it right that God is jealous for the glory, honor, and praise He deserves?**

Make sure your child understands that it would not be right for God to allow us to treat someone or something as better or greater than He is; God would be wrong to let someone or something else take first place in our hearts—in our worship or honor or praise.

Why is it right then that God's wrath (or righteous anger) is against all who forsake (forget or turn away from) him?

Do any of these truths about God give you reason to be uncomfortable or even fearful? How so? Is that a good thing or a bad thing?

02

THE UNIQUENESS OF GOD

When you talk about God, walk into church, and live your daily life, is it obvious that you truly understand that there is none like God? Who is someone you greatly admire (think is pretty great)? How would you treat that person if you met him or her? How does that compare to how you treat God?

Read the following examples from the Bible that show us how God should be treated. You may also want to look at Exodus 33:20-33.

- Isaiah's response to the vision of God high and lifted up was, *"And I said: 'Woe is me! For I am lost; for I am a man of unclean lips, and I dwell in the midst of a people of unclean lips; for my eyes have seen the King, the LORD of hosts!'"* —ISAIAH 6:5

- When David was in the wilderness, he wrote these words: *"O God, you are my God; earnestly I seek you...² I have looked upon you...beholding your power and glory. ³ Because your steadfast love is better than life, my lips will praise you, ⁴ So I will bless you as long as I live;"* (from Psalm 63:1-4).

- The psalmist tells us in Psalm 96:2-4, 9-10, *"Sing to the LORD, bless his name...³ Declare his glory...⁴ For great is the LORD, and greatly to be praised...⁹ Worship the LORD in the splendor of holiness; tremble before him...¹⁰ Say among the nations, 'The LORD reigns!'"*

- *"Oh give thanks to the LORD, for he is good, for his steadfast love endures forever! ² Let the redeemed of the LORD say so,"* —PSALM 107:1-2A

02

Have we lost some of this honor and respect for God today? How do you treat the Bible? Do you toss it around, or do you treat it as God's Holy Word? Do you give more praise to a favorite sports star than you give to the one true God? Do you treat God with casualness and familiarity (like He is just another buddy or friend)? What encourages you to treat God this way? What can you do about this? How can you treat God in a way that honors His uniqueness and greatness?

GLORIFYING GOD

Psalm 86:12 says: *"I give thanks to you, O Lord my God, with my whole heart, and I will glorify your name forever."* Can you say that your heart is like David's heart (the writer of Psalm 86)? What have you thanked God for this week? How often do you express thankfulness to God? In what ways did you praise God this week? In what ways did you take God's goodness and greatness for granted (not notice it)? How can you grow in appreciation for who God is and what He does for you each day?

WE GIVE THANKS TO YOU, O LORD

Identify and thank God for the goodness He has blessed you with this week:

_____

_____

_____

_____

_____

_____

_____

_____

_____

_____

JESUS IS GOD

Why is it true that you cannot truly know who Jesus is unless you first understand who God is? (You may want to have your children look at Colossians 1:15.)

How does God show us who He is in the Old Testament (how is His character shown)? [He shows us who He is through His mighty deeds, through His commands, through the way He treats His people, through the way He defeats His enemies...] What are some of the things you know about God from the Old Testament? When you review the list of verses we read from the Old Testament, how does Jesus show these same qualities?

INFLUENCE THE
WILL

What action or actions will you take this week to help you know and appreciate the character of God better? Think about what you have talked about and ask God to help you know how to respond and act on the truth.

FAMILY WORSHIP TIME

Read the words of the hymn "Immortal, Invisible" by Walter Chalmers Smith (*Hymns of Grace*, page 36, or find it on the internet.) As you read the words, have your children raise their hands or speak out when they hear descriptions of God's nature or character. Be sure to define and explain words that are unfamiliar. Make note of the number of attributes or names of God noted in the hymn. Sing the hymn together.

God's glorious deeds are meant to **EXCITE OUR MINDS** *to want to know more and more about God,* **MOVE OUR HEARTS** *to love and treasure Him most of all, and* **SHAPE OUR WILL** *to trust and depend on Him completely.*

03

KNOWING GOD'S GLORIOUS DEEDS

INTRODUCTION FOR PARENTS

Psalm 78:1-7 lays out a sacred responsibility and privilege for every Christian parent. We are to tell our children and the coming generations the *glorious deeds of the Lord and the wonders He has done*. As we read the narrative of Scripture, we should continually be reminded: *Who is like the one true God? No one!* God's attributes are not merely words—His divine power, wisdom, mercy, wrath, and goodness are proven true again and again as we see God act. Furthermore, the psalmist has a goal in mind in declaring these glorious deeds and works—that we and our children might set our hope in God alone. In New Testament terms: Declaring God's glorious deeds to our children is to make them wise for salvation through faith in Christ.

In reflecting on Psalm 78, Charles Spurgeon wrote the following:

> We will look forward to future generations, and endeavor to provide for their godly education. It is the duty of the church of God to maintain, in fullest vigor, every agency intended for the religious education of the young; to them we must look for the church of the future, and as we sow towards them so shall we reap. Children are to be taught to magnify the Lord; they ought to be well informed as to his wonderful doings in ages past, and should be made to know "his strength and his wonderful works he hath done." The best education is education in the best things.[1]

[1]Spurgeon, Charles Haddon. *The Treasury of David*. (Pasadena, Texas: Pilgrim Publications).

PIQUE THEIR INTEREST

Pose the following scenario:

> **Suppose a man told everyone that he was really strong. Would you simply believe him? What would determine whether or not he was believable?** [his physical stature, if you already know something of his strength, someone had witnessed him lifting something really heavy, etc.]

03

INSTRUCT THE
MIND

Introduce, read, and interact with the following Scripture.

In the last devotion, we learned about God's character—who He is and what He is like. For example, God calls Himself the "Almighty" God. That means He is all-powerful. But God doesn't just say, "I am Almighty." He also proves it to be true.

In the book of Exodus, we read of God's special people, Israel, being enslaved in Egypt. It was during this time that God appeared to Moses in the burning bush and revealed to Moses His special name "Yahweh," the LORD. This is what happened next...

> *And now, behold, the cry of the people of Israel has come to me, and I have also seen the oppression with which the Egyptians oppress them. ¹⁰ Come, I will send you to Pharaoh that you may bring my people, the children of Israel, out of Egypt."*—EXODUS 3:9-10

So Moses and his brother Aaron went to Pharaoh and said...

> *..."Thus says the LORD, the God of Israel, 'Let my people go, that they may hold a feast to me in the wilderness.'" ² But Pharaoh said, "Who is the LORD, that I should obey his voice and let*

Israel go? I do not know the LORD, and moreover,
I will not let Israel go."—EXODUS 5:1-2

Not only did Pharaoh not let Israel go upon hearing this, but he made them work even harder. But who is stronger? God or Pharaoh? Who is King over all the earth? Who will have the final say? God or Pharaoh? So God told Moses to remind Israel of God's promise to deliver them.

"...I am the LORD, and I will bring you out
from under the burdens of the Egyptians, and
I will deliver you from slavery to them, and I
will redeem you with an outstretched arm and
with great acts of judgment."—EXODUS 6:6

03

🔘 **What two-word phrase does God use three times in this verse?** ["I will."] **What does this emphasize?** [God's commitment to do what He has said]

🔘 **What did God mean by saying He would redeem Israel with great acts of judgment?** [sending plagues upon Egypt] **How many plagues did God send?** [10] **Do you remember what they were?** [frogs, gnats, flies, death of livestock, skin sores (boils on man and animals), hail, grasshoppers, darkness over the land during daytime, and death of the firstborn of Egypt]

🔘 **What was God proving to be true about the extent of His power and authority? How did God prove His power over nature? How did God prove His power over man and nations?** (Encourage responses.)

🔘 **If God is truly almighty, why did He send 10 plagues and not just one? Was it because it took 10 "tries" to get it right? Was it because Pharaoh was hard to defeat?** (Encourage responses.)

God told Pharaoh the answer to this question.

"For by now I could have put out my hand and
struck you and your people with pestilence,
and you would have been cut off from the earth.
¹⁶But for this purpose I have raised you up, to
show you my power, so that my name may be
proclaimed in all the earth."—EXODUS 9:15-16

? **What was God's purpose in sending 10 plagues?** [to show the extent of God's power so that everyone throughout the world would know that He is all-powerful]

? But that was not the end of God displaying His almighty power. **What amazing thing did God do to finally lead His people out of Egypt?** [He parted the waters of the sea so Israel could pass through on dry ground. He then returned the waters and destroyed the Egyptian armies.]

03

? **What do you think would be the response of God's people to actually seeing and experiencing this event firsthand?** (Encourage some responses.)

> *Thus the LORD saved Israel that day from the hand of the Egyptians, and Israel saw the Egyptians dead on the seashore.* [31]*Israel saw the great power that the LORD used against the Egyptians, so the people feared the LORD, and they believed in the LORD and in his servant Moses.*—EXODUS 14:30-31

? **Why would fear of the LORD and belief in Him be a right response?** (Encourage some responses.)

Immediately after the verses we previously read, we see the first recorded song in the Bible. It is a song that Israel sang to the LORD. In part it says,

> *"Who is like you, O LORD, among the gods? Who is like you, majestic in holiness, awesome in glorious deeds, doing wonders?"*—EXODUS 15:11

? **What is the significance of the question marks at the end of these two sentences? What are they meant to highlight or emphasize?** [that it's a rhetorical question with an obvious answer, no one is like the LORD, no one does deeds and wonders like Him]

? **What is the importance of God including this event in the Bible? What are we to learn from it?** (Encourage some responses.)

SUMMARY

The Bible gives us many special words that describe God's character, telling us who He is and what He is like. All of these words about God are true. God is all-powerful, wise, merciful, good, and much more. But God also wants to *show us* His power, wisdom, mercy, goodness, and more. God wants us to recall and remember His glorious deeds and the wonders He has done. When you read stories in the Bible about what God has done in the past, He is showing proof of His greatness and worth. He is proving to everyone, "I am God and there is no other. I am God. There is none like me!"

> When you read stories in the Bible about what God has done in the past, He is showing proof of His greatness and worth... This glorious God is still at work, doing wonders every moment of every day, all around us.

03

But God's glorious deeds are not just something in the past. This glorious God is still at work, doing wonders every moment of every day, all around us. God's glorious deeds can be seen in the stars that shine, a dog that plays, a delicious apple, a giant wave, a tiny ant, and a beautiful flower. But more importantly, God's glorious deeds are at work in and through the lives of His people. God's glorious deeds are meant to excite our minds to want to know more and more about God, move our hearts to love and treasure Him most of all, and shape our will to trust and depend on Him completely.

ENGAGE THE HEART

Choose one or more of the following topics to discuss.

GLORIOUS DEEDS

Make a list of some of God's glorious deeds and what they "show" about who God is [powerful, faithful, loving, just, attentive, etc.]. Explain how these deeds show these characteristics of God.

Why is it important that God back up His words with actions? What does that tell you about backing up your words with actions? Explain. (For example: Many people say: "I trust in Jesus." Should this be backed up with certain actions? Why?) **What are some ways a person can "show" that he is a true follower of Christ?**

I WILL

03

We have seen that God's statement "I will" shows His commitment to keep His Word. Read Deuteronomy 2:7 and Joshua 21:45. How do these testimonies show God's trustworthiness? What other promises has God made? Where in your own life or in the lives of others you know have you seen these promises fulfilled? Read Deuteronomy 4:9. **What warning is in this verse?** Read Deuteronomy 7:9-10. **What promise and what warning are in these verses? What do all these verses and testimonies tell you about God?**

SETTING OUR HOPE IN GOD ALONE

Are you having difficulty (a hard time) **trusting God for any circumstance or issue** (problem) **in your life? What do you think keeps you from fully trusting God?**

Make sure your child understands the temptations to sin and the tendency we have to trust in something other than in God.

What can you do about it? Is there a verse that can strengthen your trust in God in your situation?

Make sure your child does not expect to pick any promise in the Bible and think that God will fulfill it in exactly the way your child thinks He should.

THE END RESULT

Discuss the following statement, making sure your child understands each phrase:

> God's glorious deeds are meant to excite our minds to want to know more and more about God, move our hearts to love and treasure Him most of all, and shape our will to trust and depend on Him completely.

Looking at each phrase, examine how, in your heart, you truly respond. **Do you truly want to know more and more about God? How is this shown in your life? Do you truly love and treasure God most of all? How is this shown in your life? Do you truly trust and depend on God completely? How is this shown in your life? Where do you need to grow? How can you grow?**

03

INFLUENCE THE
WILL

What action or actions can you take this week to see who God is, to treasure Him more, to trust Him more, or to proclaim His name? What action or actions can you take to grow in faith this week?

FAMILY WORSHIP TIME

Read the words of the hymn "How Great Thou Art" by Stuart K. Hine (*Hymns of Grace*, 5, or find it on the internet). Make sure to define and explain words that are unfamiliar.

What specific wonders of God do the first two verses focus on? What glorious deed of God is emphasized in verse 3? Why is this important? What future glorious deed is highlighted in verse 4?

Sing the hymn together.

God created us—either as male or female, boy or girl— **IN HIS IMAGE** *and likeness. We were created this way for a very special purpose—to glorify God in everything we think, feel, say, and do.*

KNOWING GOD'S PURPOSE FOR HIS PEOPLE

INTRODUCTION FOR PARENTS

In our day, self-expression has become the rule of the land. Contemporary culture would have us believe that each individual has the freedom and right to define who they are and how others are to perceive them. Even the age-old boundaries of gender—male and female—are outwardly being destroyed, making way for self-identification, no matter how absurd. It is within this cultural climate that God's Word shines forth like lightning, bringing sharp clarity and divine authority. God made us, and God owns us. God declares our essence and being, and God defines our purpose. There is no negotiating. He is our Creator, and we are His dependent creatures.

The first question of the Westminster Catechism gets to the heart of the matter:

> **Q. 1. What is the chief and highest end of man?**[1]

The answer:

> **A. Man's chief and highest end is to glorify God, and fully to enjoy him forever.**

This question and answer rightly point us Godward as we seek to understand our essence, identity, and purpose. It fundamentally grounds us in what is unique about us—

....
[1] Westminster Larger Catechism, Question 1.

that we have been created to reflect and image forth the awesome majesty and worth of our Creator. And, in that imaging forth, we are to pursue the highest purpose: glorifying God! We glorify God by giving Him the honor, respect, love, devotion, obedience, and worship He so rightly deserves. It is only by embracing this call that we will be able to experience true, lasting joy.

PIQUE THEIR INTEREST

Have everyone briefly name a favorite piece of technology or invention and one or two reasons for liking it.

04

Could an animal have designed and built this? Why not?

Do you think that the designer of each invention had a specific use in mind? Would the inventor be pleased if someone used his design for the wrong purpose? For example, someone using a laptop computer as a dinner plate. **Can you think of one way the invention you named could be misused in an absurd, silly, or even dangerous way?**

Encourage each family member to give one or two responses. You may need to give them one or two examples to get them thinking in the right direction, such as using a sports car as a refrigerator, using a phone to hit a baseball, etc.

INSTRUCT THE MIND

Ask the questions, and read and interact with the Scriptures.

Think now of human beings. **Have we been designed and created? By whom? Where in the Bible do we first see God creating all things?** [Genesis 1]

Quickly read the following Scripture portions from Genesis 1:

In the beginning, God created the heavens and the earth. (verse 1)
And God said, "Let there be light," (verse 3)
*And God said, "Let there be an expanse in the midst
of the waters..."* (verse 6)
And God said, "Let the waters...be gathered together..." (verse 9)
And God said, "Let the earth sprout vegetation..." (verse 11)

What is the key phrase in each day of creation? ["And God said"]
Genesis 1 continues with this pattern: God speaking creation into
existence in six days. God creating everything out of nothing, all
by Himself, showing that He alone is the Designer and Creator.
But when we get to verses 26 and 27, something unique happens.

04

*Then God said, "Let us make man in our image, after
our likeness..."* [27] *So God created man in his own
image, in the image of God he created him; male
and female he created them.*—GENESIS 1:26A, 27

What is the significance of being designed and created in
God's image and likeness? (What does it mean to be designed?)
(Encourage some responses. You may want help a younger child by
referring to a doll being made in the likeness of a real baby, or a toy
truck being made in the likeness of a real truck. For an older child,
you may ask how a human being
is different from an animal in the
ways it thinks, feels, and acts.)

**What are the two distinct image
bearers in this verse?** [male and
female] **Why is this an important
distinction?** [God has decided
that all human beings are either
male or female. God creating
us either as male or female
is "fixed"—we cannot decide
this for ourselves.]

To be made in the image of God—
either as male or female—means
to be made "like" God in certain
ways so that we are able to "do"

God created us with
minds like God's own
mind so that we can
think, reason, study,
and understand;
hearts like His own
heart so that we
can feel certain
emotions, such as
joy, sorrow, and love;
and wills like God's
own will so that we
can make choices
and decisions.

certain things and relate to God in special ways. For example, God created us with minds like God's own mind so that we can think, reason, study, and understand. That is why the inventions we mentioned earlier are all designed by people and not animals. We have been given minds that can design and create things—reflecting God's creativity. God also created us with hearts like His own heart so that we can feel certain emotions, such as joy, sorrow, and love. God created us with wills like God's own will so that we can make choices and decisions in what we say and do.

Read the following Scripture and instruct your child to listen carefully for words or phrases that point to something we do with our mind (thoughts), heart (feelings), or will (choices, actions). If you like, you could instruct your child to raise his or her hand when you read a specific example.

04

> *With my whole heart I seek you;*
> *let me not wander from your commandments!*
> *¹¹I have stored up your word in my heart,*
> *that I might not sin against you.*
> *¹²Blessed are you, O LORD; teach me your statutes!*
> *¹³With my lips I declare all the rules of your mouth.*
> *¹⁴In the way of your testimonies I delight*
> *as much as in all riches.*
> *¹⁵I will meditate on your precepts*
> *and fix my eyes on your ways.*
> *¹⁶I will delight in your statutes;*
> *I will not forget your word.—PSALM 119:10-16*

❓ **Would animals be able to think, feel, and act in these ways? Why not?** [They have not been created in God's image.] **Why do you think all the thoughts, feelings, words, and actions of the psalmist are directed toward, or are responding to God and His Word?** (Encourage some responses.) **Do these verses show a special kind of relationship between the psalmist and God? How would you describe this relationship?** [affection, admiration, commitment, confidence or trust, appreciation, respect]

We have been designed and created to be able to experience and express these kinds of thoughts, feelings, words, and actions in response to who God is and what He is like. The Bible gives us a special word to summarize the great purpose for which we were created.

Before reading the Scriptures that follow, instruct your children to listen very carefully for a special, seven-letter word that is repeated in each verse.

You who fear the LORD, praise him!
All you offspring of Jacob, glorify him,
and stand in awe of him...—PSALM 22:23B

All the nations you have made shall
come and worship before you, O Lord,
and shall glorify your name.—PSALM 86:9

I give thanks to you, O Lord my God,
with my whole heart, and I will glorify
your name forever.—PSALM 86:12

You are not your own, ²⁰*for you were*
bought with a price. So glorify God in
your body.—1 CORINTHIANS 6:19B-20

04

What is the special seven-letter word found in each verse? [glorify] **Based on these verses and the ones we read before, what does it mean to "glorify" God?** [fear Him, stand in awe of Him, gives thanks to Him, love Him with your whole heart, not sin against Him, etc.] **Why would it be important to know that glorifying God is our main purpose in life?** (Refer to the "Pique Their Interest" illustration at the beginning of this devotion time.) **Do you think a person could ever be truly happy apart from doing what he or she was created to do? Why not?**

In Psalm 16, David described his relationship with God this way:

You make known to me the path of life; in your
presence there is fullness of joy; at your right
hand are pleasures forevermore.—PSALM 16:11

What does David say that God has made known to him? [the path of life] **What do you think he meant by this?** [For example, there is a certain way that leads to everlasting life with God. In the New Testament, we see that it is only through trusting in Jesus.] **What has David found to be true of being in God's presence and having a close, special relationship with God?** [It brings fullness of joy and happiness forever.]

SUMMARY

God is the Designer and Creator of all things. Therefore, God rightly owns and rules all things and decides their purpose. God created human beings in a unique way. God created us—either as male or female, boy or girl—in His image and likeness. We were created this way for a very special purpose—to glorify God in everything we think, feel, say, and do. This allows us to have very special and close relationship with God. Glorifying God is the only thing that will make us truly happy. If we try to live for a purpose other than glorifying God, it will end in

> **Glorifying God is the only thing that will make us truly happy. If we try to live for a purpose other than glorifying God, it will end in frustration and disappointment.**

frustration and disappointment. There is a "path" that God has made known to us—the way to glorify Him and enjoy Him forever. In the coming devotions, we will be learning more about that path.

04

ENGAGE THE HEART

Choose one or more of the following topics to discuss.

GOD, THE OWNER AND DESIGNER

Why is it so important to understand that God is the Designer and Creator of all things? What does this tell you about man?

God has designed fish to live in water. What would happen if a fish could decide to live apart from God's design (like in a tree)? What does this obvious example tell you about living apart from God's design? What does this tell you about why you can trust God's design?

IN HIS IMAGE

God created us with hearts that can feel certain emotions. **Why is this a good thing? Why is this a hard thing? What kinds of things does God rejoice in? What kinds of things does God sorrow over?** (Be specific.) **Does your heart rejoice in the things that God rejoices in? Does it sorrow over the things God sorrows over? What does this show you about yourself and where you need to grow?**

God created us with wills so that we can make choices and decisions. This is a great blessing, but also a great responsibility. Explain this statement. **What are some of the choices you made this week? Do they reflect what God wills?** Explain.

04

CREATED MALE AND FEMALE

Your gender was determined by God in the womb as either male or female.[2] **What are some of the lies that our world tells us about gender? What is the result of living apart from God's gender design? How is living apart from God's design rebellion? What does attempting to**

> *I give thanks to you, O Lord my God, with my whole heart, and I will glorify your name forever.*
> PSALM 86:12

change God's design say about man? What does it say about how our society thinks about God? How can you be a voice for truth in a confused world? Will this be popular? Should that matter to you? (See John 15:18-19.)

Living as God created you brings the greatest joy. If you are a male (boy), what things can you do to reflect God's design in making you male? (What can he be doing now to grow into manhood and develop skills to lead and provide?) **If you are a female (girl), what things can you do to reflect God's design in making you female?** (What can she be doing now to grow into womanhood and develop nurturing and helping skills?)

---

[2]In extremely rare cases, genetic mutations may result in a child being born with both male and female anatomy. Decisions regarding the child's gender in these cases must be made with medical knowledge, godly wisdom, compassion, and humble caution. It is a reminder that this present world is fallen, under a curse, and groaning as we await the redemption of our bodies.

OUR GREAT PURPOSE

What does it mean to glorify God in what we think? Feel? Say? Do? (Be specific.) What did you do this week that brought glory to God? What did you do this week that did not bring glory to God? Explain. Which thoughts, feelings, conversations, and actions brought you more joy? What does this tell you? How can you more intentionally live in a way that brings glory to God?

THE PATH OF LIFE

There are only two paths in life—the path of life and the path of destruction. **According to Psalm 16:11, how can you tell if you are on the path of life?**

04

Be sure your child understands that those on the path of life enjoy being in God's presence...They love to fellowship with God—read His Word, pray, worship Him in church. They love the things God loves—they hate evil and cling to what is good. They rejoice in the things that God rejoices in and want to glorify Him, etc.

How does a person get on the path to life? (Refer your child to John 14:6 and discuss this verse.)

Think of an older person you have known for at least a few years. **How does this person's life bring glory to God or show a rebellion against God? Does this person demonstrate joy?** Explain. (You may want to share this person's testimony with your child.)

> *You make known to me the path of life; in your presence there is fullness of joy; at your right hand are pleasures forevermore.*
> PSALM 16:11
>
> *Jesus said to him, "I am the way, and the truth, and the life. No one comes to the Father except through me."*
> JOHN 14:6

INFLUENCE THE
WILL

What action or actions will you take this week to live according to God's design and to bring glory to Him? If you are not on the path of life, what action or actions can you take this week to seriously consider the direction of your life?

FAMILY WORSHIP TIME

04

Read the words of the song "We Will Glorify" by Twila Paris (*Hymns of Grace*, 97, or find it on the internet). As you read the song, note the different ways God is described. **What is the significance of each? Why does each attribute of God call for a right response?** Note the types of responses giving glory to God. Sing the song together.

The Old Testament is a
TESTIMONY OF THE FAITHFULNESS OF GOD.
It is a record book of promises made and promises kept.

KNOWING GOD'S PROMISES

INTRODUCTION FOR PARENTS

The Old Testament narrative is an amazing testimony to the faithfulness of God in bringing about His sovereign purposes. Furthermore, throughout the varied stories, themes, and events of the Old Testament, we see one overarching storyline—the progressive revelation of God choosing and redeeming a people for Himself, a people who are to be set apart, "holy" to the LORD. A people bound, guided, and protected by the promises of God. Promises *made* by God are always shown to be promises *fulfilled* by God. God always does what His says He will do. No one is able to thwart His purposes. All creation, whether rock, water, bird, or man, serves God's grand design and plans.

It is within this context that children can better understand and appreciate the Gospel. The Gospel is the culmination of God's promises and purposes for His chosen people. Every promise in the Old Testament provides an unshakable foundation for understanding and trusting in the Gospel. Every Old Testament promise points forward to the meaning and necessity of the perfect work of Christ. God's good and wise providence over the people of Israel is the same providence acting to save His sinful people through the death of His beloved Son. Recounting these past promises is meant to give God's people confidence for the future as we anticipate Jesus' return, our resurrection unto eternal life, and the establishment of His everlasting kingdom.

PIQUE THEIR INTEREST

Ask everyone,

> Suppose I promised you a special dessert if you eat all your vegetables at dinnertime. **Do you believe that this is a promise I would keep? Why or why not? Would this promise motivate you to eat your vegetables, even vegetables you don't really like?**
>
> Now suppose I promised to give you one million dollars after dinner. **Do you believe that this is a promise I would be able to keep? Why or why not? If I were able to do this, would this promise motivate you even more to eat your vegetables?**

INSTRUCT THE MIND

05

Introduce, read, and interact with the following Scriptures:

The Bible is filled with promises from God. If you read the Bible very carefully, you will be able to recognize these promises. God's promises are important because they show us something about His character—who He is and what He is like. And they also show us how He acts toward people—especially His chosen people. We are going to read just a few of these promises from the Old Testament.

> *"For behold, I will bring a flood of waters upon the earth to destroy all flesh in which is the breath of life under heaven. Everything that is on the earth shall die. ¹⁸But I will establish my covenant with you, and you shall come into the ark, you, your sons, your wife, and your sons' wives with you."*—GENESIS 6:17-18

❓ **Who was God speaking to?** [Noah] **What two important things was God promising to do?** (Look for the phrase, "I will.") [God will bring a flood and destroy all living things. God will establish a covenant with Noah and save his family.] **Do you remember why God promised to destroy the earth?** [because of the wickedness and evil of man—see verse 5] **What does this tell us about God's character?** [God's holiness is seen in His hatred of evil. God is right to punish evil.] **What does God's promise to Noah tell us about God's character?** [possible response: He is loving and merciful to His people] **Would sending a flood be something anyone could do? Why not? Did God keep His promise?**

> *"...I am the LORD, and I will bring you out*
> *from under the burdens of the Egyptians,*
> *and I will deliver you from slavery to them,*
> *and I will redeem you with an outstretched arm*
> *and with great acts of judgment."*—EXODUS 6:6

We looked at this verse in a previous devotion. God promises three things for His people Israel in this verse—"I will...I will...I will..." Did God do all three things? Yes, God did just as He promised. He freed them from bondage and slavery in Egypt and led them to the land He had promised them.

05

These are just two examples of God making and keeping promises to certain people at a specific time and place. If you read the Old Testament carefully, you will find hundreds of examples like these. It shows a pattern: God made a promise. God kept a promise. God made a promise. God kept a promise. Over and over, and over again, God is proven to be faithful—He always does what He says He will do.

Why is this important for you and me to know and understand? [God is always dependable. I should trust Him at all times. God is all-powerful, and nothing is too hard for Him. God is good, loving, and kind toward His people. God is still keeping His promises. It's dangerous to oppose God—you will not win. God's warnings should be taken seriously.]

Knowing and seeing God's faithfulness is important because God is still at work keeping His promises. **Can you recall some promises from the Bible— including any New Testament promises?** (Spend a few moments recalling some

> **God made a promise. God kept a promise. Over and over again, God is proven to be faithful—He always does what He says He will do.**

promises you and your children have learned, even if you cannot recite the entire verse or remember the reference. Or you could use one or more of the verses listed below.)

for the LORD knows the way of the righteous,
but the way of the wicked will perish.—PSALM 1:6

"Have I not commanded you?
Be strong and courageous. Do not be frightened,
and do not be dismayed, for the LORD your God
is with you wherever you go."—JOSHUA 1:9

And we know that for those who love God all
things work together for good, for those who are
called according to his purpose.—ROMANS 8:28

For "everyone who calls on the name
of the Lord will be saved."—ROMANS 10:13

Jesus said…"I am the resurrection and the life.
Whoever believes in me, though he die,
yet shall he live."—JOHN 11:25

05

Can God be depended on to keep these promises, too? What should give us confidence to believe in these promises, too? [God's past faithfulness—He has kept every single promise He has made.]

SUMMARY

The Old Testament is a testimony of the faithfulness of God. It is a record book of promises made and promises kept. Some of these promises are wonderful as they promise good things for those who trust in the LORD God and walk in His ways. Some promises are terrifying as they show God's judgment on everyone who would oppose Him and do things their own way instead of God's way. Some promises were given to a certain people at a specific place and time.

These promises prove to us that God is trustworthy in all He says. They show that He is good, righteous, and holy (perfect) in all His ways. They show that God loves, cares for, and protects His people at all times. They show that no one and nothing can prevent God from keeping His promises. This is true today, and it will be true in the future, too. God will never change. As we read the New Testament, we can see even more promises, including the greatest promise of all—complete forgiveness of sin and the promise of eternal life with God through trusting in Jesus. God is faithful. He will do it!

ENGAGE THE HEART

Choose one or more of the following topics to discuss.

EVIDENCES OF GOD'S FAITHFULNESS

The Bible is full of examples of God keeping His promises. Name some of these evidences of His faithfulness. **What are some examples of God's faithfulness in your life, or in the life of our family?**

Spend some time remembering God's goodness to your family and thank Him for His faithfulness.

05

EVIDENCES OF GOD'S FAITHFULNESS
How we have seen God be faithful and good to our family:

_____

_____

_____

_____

_____

_____

_____

NO ONE CAN THWART GOD'S PURPOSES

Can you think of examples in the Bible of man's inability to thwart God's purposes? What does that tell you about God? How can this give you confidence for today? Can you think of an example in your life, the life of our family, or the life of someone else where God especially showed His power (His purposes could not be thwarted)? Why should this give you great confidence and security? What would it mean if God's purposes could be thwarted?

RECOUNTING GOD'S PROMISES

In Psalm 77, the psalmist (Asaph) was very discouraged. After expressing his discouragement, he said, *"Then I said, 'I will appeal to this, to the years of the right hand of the Most High.' ¹¹I will remember the deeds of the LORD; yes, I will remember your wonders of old."*—PSALM 77:10-11. He then tells some of God's deeds. Why does the psalmist do this? What can you learn from this?

05

Are you discouraged about anything, or is there any trouble or problem in your life? What are some of the deeds and promises you can remember in order to encourage your soul?

When you remember God's promises and His mighty deeds, you are "speaking to your soul," rather than "listening to your emotions." **Why is this so important?** (You might want to look at Romans 12:2 with your child.) **What are obstacles to** (what keeps you from) **speaking to your soul? What can you do about that?**

CONFIDENCE IN GOD

How can you tell if you have confidence in God?

You may want to discuss with your child what worry, fear, discouragement, etc. tell us about how much confidence we have in God's purposes and His ability to carry them out for the good of His children.

What do your emotions indicate (tell) about how much confidence you have in God? What does your mind tell you about God's trustworthiness? How can you get your heart to agree with your mind? Are there any habits you need to develop? Are there any habits you need to put an end to?

TWO IMPORTANT PROMISES

Read Psalm 1:6 again.

> *for the LORD knows the way of the righteous, but*
> *the way of the wicked will perish.* —PSALM 1:6

What two important promises are in this verse? What assurance do you have that God will keep these promises? There are only two paths to choose in life. Do you know what path you are on? How do you know this?

Help your child to seriously consider whether he is truly a believer and following the Lord.

INFLUENCE THE WILL

05

What action or actions can you take to memorize some of the promises, speak to your soul, grow in your confidence toward God, or consider the path you are on?

FAMILY WORSHIP TIME

Read the words of the hymn, "Every Promise of Your Word" by Keith Getty and Stuart Townend (*Hymns of Grace*, 363, or find it on the internet). Explain any difficult words or phrases. Talk about what it means to "stand on" a promise (e.g., to take hold of it, trust and depend on it, cling to it, etc.) **Why do you think the hymn writers repeatedly use the phrase, "...of Your Word"?** Challenge an older child to recall specific verses that are reflected in the hymn. Sing the hymn together.

When we **HONOR, RESPECT,**
and **REVERENCE GOD**
as we should, it brings about
true, lasting joy in our
lives—fullness of joy and
pleasures evermore!

HONORING THE MOST HIGH GOD

06

INTRODUCTION FOR PARENTS

Here are some words from Jerry Bridges that the contemporary evangelical church desperately needs to hear and consider:

> It is impossible to be devoted to God if one's heart is not filled with the fear of God. It is this profound sense of veneration and honor, reverence and awe that draws forth from our hearts the worship and adoration that characterizes true devotion to God.
>
> ...In our day we must begin to recover a sense of awe and profound reverence for God. We must begin to view Him once again in the infinite majesty that alone belongs to Him who is the Creator and Supreme Ruler of the entire universe. There is an infinite gap in worth and dignity between God the Creator and man the creature, even though man has been created in the image of God. The fear of God is a heartfelt recognition of this gap...[1]

Parents are on the frontlines of promoting a proper honor for God in the lives of their children. We must teach our children a biblical reverence and awe of the Holy One. We must teach and live out before our children what it means that "the fear of the LORD" is the beginning of knowledge and wisdom. (See Proverbs 1:7 and Proverbs 9:10.)

....
[1]Bridges, Jerry. *The Practice of Godliness*. (Colorado Springs, Colo.: NavPress, 1983, 1996), 20, 21.

06 PIQUE THEIR INTEREST

Have everyone imagine that your family received a personal invitation to visit the Queen of England at Buckingham Palace.

Would play clothes, or dirty and torn work clothes, be appropriate? Why not? How would you address the Queen when you met her? Would you say something like, "Hey, Lizzy! How are you doing"? Why wouldn't that be appropriate? And suppose she invited us to sit down and chat for a few minutes, would you take out your phone and chat with a friend instead? Would you run around the room and jump on the furniture?

There is something called "etiquette" or "protocol" that should be used when meeting a person of high rank. For example, you should address the queen as, "Your majesty." You should quietly pay attention to what she says and put away other distractions. You would treat the palace as a special room, and not simply a playground.

INSTRUCT THE MIND

Introduce, read, and interact with the following Scripture.

After the people of Israel left Egypt, God led them through the wilderness to the land of Sinai. In Sinai there was a mountain— Mount Sinai. It was at this place where God issued a special invitation. He was going to come down and meet with His people, and speak to them through Moses.

> *...The LORD called to [Moses] out of the mountain, saying, "Thus you shall say to the house of Jacob, and tell the people of Israel: ⁴ 'You yourselves have seen what I did to the Egyptians, and how I bore you on eagles' wings and brought you to myself. ⁵ Now therefore, if you will indeed obey my voice and keep my covenant, you shall be my treasured*

06

possession among all peoples, for all the earth is mine; ⁶and you shall be to me a kingdom of priests and a holy nation.'"—EXODUS 19:3-6

...And the LORD said to Moses, "Behold, I am coming to you in a thick cloud, that the people may hear when I speak with you, and may also believe you forever"...¹⁰..."Go to the people and consecrate them today and tomorrow, and let them wash their garments ¹¹and be ready for the third day. For on the third day the LORD will come down on Mount Sinai in the sight of all the people. ¹²And you shall set limits for the people all around, saying, 'Take care not to go up into the mountain or touch the edge of it. Whoever touches the mountain shall be put to death. ¹³...When the trumpet sounds a long blast, they shall come up to the mountain." ¹⁴So Moses went down from the mountain to the people and consecrated the people...—EXODUS 19:9-14

❓ **God told Moses to "consecrate" the people before this meeting. What does that mean?** (Washing their garments or clothing gives us a small clue.) To consecrate means to "set apart for a special use or purpose." It means getting your mind, heart, and body—even your clothing—ready to meet with God.

❓ **What other special instructions did God give concerning the mountain?** [to put limits—a boundary—around it that the people should not cross] **What did God say was the consequence if someone went up the mountain, or even tried to touch the edge of it?** [He or she would be put to death.] **What's the big deal? Isn't that a rather harsh penalty?** (Encourage a few general responses at this point.)

Here is what happened on the day God's presence came down upon the mountain:

On the morning of the third day there were thunders and lightnings and a thick cloud on the mountain and a very loud trumpet blast, so that all the people in the camp trembled.

06

> *¹⁷ Then Moses brought the people out of the camp to meet God, and they took their stand at the foot of the mountain. ¹⁸ Now Mount Sinai was wrapped in smoke because the LORD had descended on it in fire. The smoke of it went up like the smoke of a kiln, and the whole mountain trembled greatly. ¹⁹ And as the sound of the trumpet grew louder and louder, Moses spoke, and God answered him in thunder. ²⁰ The LORD came down on Mount Sinai, to the top of the mountain...—EXODUS 19:16-20*

Was this a casual or ordinary type of meeting? Do you think the people of Israel were yawning, whispering to their friends, and making jokes? Why not? What kinds of thoughts and feelings may they have experienced? [amazement, awe, fear, excitement, etc.]

I am going to read some verses that give us a certain type of "etiquette" or "protocol" that should be used toward God. The people of Israel probably experienced all of these when God came down on Mount Sinai.

> *For great is the LORD, and greatly to be praised, and he is to be feared above all gods.*—1 CHRONICLES 16:25

The LORD is to be what? [praised and feared] Why? [because He is great]

> *Let all the earth fear the LORD; let all the inhabitants of the world stand in awe of him! ⁹ For he spoke, and it came to be; he commanded, and it stood firm.*—PSALM 33:8-9

What are the inhabitants of the world to do? [fear the LORD and stand in awe of Him] Why? [He created everything, and rules everything by His command.]

> *The LORD reigns; let the peoples tremble! He sits enthroned upon the cherubim; let the earth quake!*—PSALM 99:1

What are the people to do in response to the LORD? [tremble] Why? [He sits enthroned. He rules over the heavenly beings.]

06

Oh come, let us worship and bow down;
let us kneel before the LORD, our Maker!—PSALM 95:6

How are we to act toward God? [worship, bow down, and kneel before Him] **Why?** [He is the LORD, the one true God, and our Maker.]

For the LORD, the Most High, is to be feared,
a great king over all the earth.—PSALM 47:2

The LORD is to be what? [feared] **Why?** [He is the Most High, and King over all the earth.]

...let us offer to God acceptable worship,
with reverence and awe, 29 *for our God is*
a consuming fire.—HEBREWS 12:28B-29

According to these verses, should we treat God in a casual manner? A silly manner? A bored manner? A defiant manner? Why not? (Encourage some thoughtful responses. See if they can recall some of God's attributes in order to see that God is worthy to be treated with the highest respect.)

SUMMARY

The LORD is the one true God. His greatness and worth far outrank anything or anyone else. He is the Most High God. Therefore, God deserves to be treated with the greatest honor and respect. He is not to be treated in an ordinary or casual type of manner. God is to be feared. That means we are to have a deep reverence for Him, recognizing and understanding His

> He is the Most High God. Therefore, God deserves to be treated with the greatest honor and respect.

matchless authority and power, and then gladly submit and devote ourselves to Him. Our thoughts, feelings, words, and actions should demonstrate this reverence toward God. He is not to be treated lightly or trifled with. Furthermore, when we honor, respect, and reverence God as we should, it brings about true, lasting joy in our lives—fullness of joy and pleasures evermore!

06

ENGAGE THE
HEART

Choose one or more of the following topics to discuss.

A TREASURED POSSESSION

Look again at Exodus 19:5-6. **What is the condition placed on Israel in this verse? What is the promise God made to them?**

> *"...if you will indeed obey my voice and keep my covenant, you shall be my treasured possession among all peoples, for all the earth is mine; ⁶and you shall be to me a kingdom of priests and a holy nation.'..."*

Now read 1 Peter 2:9-10. God is still calling people to be His people today—to be His treasured possession, a kingdom of priests, and a holy nation. **What is the meaning of these three descriptions of His people? If you are a Christian, how can you reflect this identity** (show that this is what you are)?

CONSECRATED TO GOD

What does it mean for you to be consecrated to God or "set apart"? (Think very practically.) **When you go to worship God on Sunday mornings, how can you get your mind, heart, and body ready to meet with God? Is there anything you need to change in your Sunday morning routine?**

In what ways can you get yourself ready to meet with God each day? (Give some practical suggestions.²) **Are there things you need to change, add, or omit (drop) from your daily life?**

Why would the consequence of touching the mountain be so severe? What does this say about God? What does this say about man? What could be in the heart of a person who was

---

²Parents, you may want your child to think about time, place, content of their Bible time, habits that need to be established or dropped, attitudes, etc.

bold enough to try to touch the mountain? How is this relevant (what is the meaning) **for us today?**

06

---

8 TIPS TO BE PREPARED FOR SUNDAY

1. **BE PREPARED FOR WORSHIP.** On Saturday night, lay out clothes, gather church bags and practice memory verses. Keep Sunday breakfast simple and leave the house with time to spare.

2. **BE A ROLE MODEL FOR YOUR CHILDREN.** Start your morning with a positive attitude, a cheerful tone, and a heart for worship.

3. **WALK YOUR CHILD THROUGH THE SERVICE BEFORE IT STARTS.** Talk through what will happen during the service and pray together.

4. **PRAY FOR YOUR CHILD.** Pray that your child will learn to participate and listen attentively, and that his heart would be inclined to the Lord.

5. **ENCOURAGE YOUR CHILD TO PARTICIPATE IN THE SERVICE.** Teach your child songs at home, sit and stand at the appropriate times, etc.

6. **HELP YOUR CHILD BECOME AN ACTIVE SERMON LISTENER.** Encourage your younger child to draw a picture of something from the sermon or older child to copy your notes or take their own notes.

7. **STRETCH YOUR CHILD'S ABILITY TO SIT STILL AND BE ATTENTIVE.** Be firm and affirm positive behavior.

8. **TALK ABOUT SERVICES ON THE WAY HOME.** Ask if your child has any questions, encourage him to share drawings or notes, discuss the service, and encourage application as appropriate.

HONORING GOD

The verses we read from 1 Chronicles, Psalms, and Hebrews showed many reactions to God—amazement, awe, fear, excitement, trembling, respect, worship, etc. **Is there a time when you felt any of these emotions or reactions to God? Explain the situation and why you reacted this way. Would you like to respond to God like this more often? What would encourage this?**

In what ways is God so much greater than you? Why is it easy to forget this? What does treating God in a casual manner look like? What kinds of things in your life encourage you to treat God casually—to treat Him as unimportant or not special? What can you do about this?

Do you have friends who encourage you to honor God? What can you do to develop these kinds of friendships?

A CONSUMING FIRE

06

Read Hebrews 12:28b-29 again.

> *...let us offer to God acceptable worship, with reverence and awe, ²⁹ for our God is a consuming fire.*—HEBREWS 12:28B-29

What does it mean that God is a "consuming fire"?

Make sure your child understands that, in this context, it means that God expects undivided worship. He will not accept being in "second place." He wants wholehearted worship and will not share that worship with anyone or anything else.

What kinds of things get in the way of worshipping the one true God alone? What personally pulls you away from worshipping only God? Is there anything in your life you need to turn away from?

Help your child to understand that there are many things in life that compete for our affections. Idolatry is not just bowing down to statues of gods, but is allowing something else to consume our heart for God.

INFLUENCE THE
WILL

What action or actions can you take this week to honor God, see Him as awesome, or get rid of something that distracts you from honoring God?

FAMILY WORSHIP TIME

Read the words of the song "Behold Our God" by Ryan, Jonathan, and Meghan Baird, and Stephen Altrogge (*Hymns of Grace*, 126, or find it on the internet). **Why do many of the stanzas end with a question mark? How do these convey that God's greatness and worth is far above us? What do the writers highlight in verse 3? Why is this important? Listen to or hum the tune of the song. How does the tune set an appropriate tone for the words? Why is this important? Sing the song together.**

MEETING GOD EVERY DAY

Think through your family's average day. Are you "set apart"? What do you need to change, add, or omit from your routine to meet God every day?

MORNING

DAY

EVENING

God's commands are meant to lead us to our **GREATEST TREASURE** and reward— God Himself.

TREASURING GOD MOST

INTRODUCTION FOR PARENTS

We tend to ascribe love to so many things. In the same conversation we may state, "I love ice cream," and "I love my children." Yet we instinctively know that the latter "love" carries a weight and meaning far beyond the former. Therefore, it is important to clarify the meaning of love, especially in light of the greatest command:

> *"And you shall love the Lord your God with all your heart and with all your soul and with all your mind and with all your strength."*—MARK 12:30

Love for God is to be ultimate, and it should involve every aspect of our being—every thought, emotion, attitude, word, and action. There are to be no competitors for our total devotion. God is worthy of our greatest affections. One way in which to communicate this type of love, especially to children, is to speak in terms of *treasuring* God most. As Jesus said, "where your treasure is, there your heart will be also" (Matthew 6:21). Therefore, we could define loving God as knowing, feeling, and treating God as your greatest treasure. Treasuring God in this manner is the only thing that will ultimately satisfy the soul. It is within this context that we realize that the command to love God most is not only our greatest duty, but also our greatest delight.

PIQUE THEIR INTEREST

Pose the following scenarios for discussion:

07

Suppose I brought home your favorite food for dinner and commanded you to come to the dinner table to eat it. Should you obey my command? Why? How would you feel about obeying it? Why?

Suppose I told you that a treasure chest filled with gold was buried in the backyard. I told you to get a shovel and start digging for it. **Should you obey me? What would be your attitude as you obeyed?**

Sometimes we think of commands as things to be obeyed grudgingly—I have to do this, but I don't want to do this. People sometimes look at God's commands this way. But, as our two pretend commands showed, there are commands that are not only our duty to obey, but also a delight to obey. They are commands that are meant to lead us to something wonderful.

INSTRUCT THE MIND

Read the following summary statement reviewing the key concepts from the previous devotion.

In the previous devotion, we learned that the LORD God deserves to be treated with the greatest honor and respect. He is not to be treated in an ordinary or casual type of manner. God is to be feared as we recognize and understand His authority and power—He is God and we are not. We should gladly submit and devote ourselves to Him. That includes obeying His commands. The Bible is filled, from beginning to end, with God's commands. Today, we are going to look at just one of these commands—the most important one.

Introduce, read, and interact with the following Scriptures.

When God came down to meet with the people of Israel on Mount Sinai, it was for the purpose of giving His people His special law and commands—most importantly, the Ten Commandments. Remember what had taken place before this. God had miraculously freed them from slavery in Egypt, fed them and given them water in the wilderness, protected them, and shown Himself good and faithful toward them.

07

After giving Israel the Ten Commandments on Mount Sinai, God told Moses to say this to Israel:

> *"Now this is the commandment—the statutes and*
> *the rules—that the LORD your God commanded*
> *me to teach you, that you may do them in the land*
> *to which you are going over, to possess it,*
> *² that you may fear the LORD your God, you and your*
> *son and your son's son, by keeping all his statutes*
> *and his commandments, which I command you, all*
> *the days of your life, and that your days may be long.*
> *³ Hear therefore, O Israel, and be careful to do*
> *them, that it may go well with you, and that you*
> *may multiply greatly, as the LORD, the God of*
> *your fathers, has promised you, in a land flowing*
> *with milk and honey."—DEUTERONOMY 6:1-3*

⍰ **According to these verses, how were the people of Israel to show that they feared the LORD?** [by keeping His commandments]

The next verses add something very important...

> *"Hear, O Israel: The LORD our God, the LORD is one.*
> *⁵ You shall love the LORD your God with all your*
> *heart and with all your soul and with all your might.*
> *⁶ And these words that I command you today*
> *shall be on your heart."—DEUTERONOMY 6:4-6*

⍰ **What is the important command in these verses?** [to love the LORD with all your heart, soul, and might] **What term is repeated three times in verse 5?** [all]

In the New Testament, Jesus says that this is the greatest commandment of all. It is the most important commandment for us to obey.

07

❓ **How would you summarize love toward God that includes all your heart, all your soul, and all your might?** [Possible responses: It is a heartfelt love and devotion to God. It is to be greater and stronger than any other affection you have toward anything or anyone else.]

In the book of Psalms, we are given some examples of how this kind of love for God is shown in a person's life. Here are three examples:

> *One thing have I asked of the LORD, that will I seek after: that I may dwell in the house of the LORD all the days of my life, to gaze upon the beauty of the LORD and to inquire in his temple.*—PSALM 27:4

❓ **What was the one thing David wanted more than anything else?** [to be with God and see His beauty] **Of all the things in the world, why would David want this one thing?** (Encourage some responses.)

> *As a deer pants for flowing streams, so pants my soul for you, O God. ²My soul thirsts for God, for the living God.*—PSALM 42:1-2A

❓ **Have you ever been really, really thirsty? What does a really thirsty person want more than anything else? How can do these verses show us what it means to love God most?** [Possible response: You long for Him and seek after Him more than anything or anyone else, because you need Him most of all.]

> *Whom have I in heaven but you? And there is nothing on earth that I desire besides you. ²⁶My flesh and my heart may fail, but God is the strength of my heart and my portion forever.*—PSALM 73:25-26

❓ **In verse 25, what is the psalmist saying about the worth of God in his life?** [Nothing else compares to his desire for God.] **What does it mean when he says that God is his "portion forever"?** [God Himself is his treasure and reward.]

❓ **Do these three examples show merely an outward expression of love for God—just saying words..."I love You"? How do they show the meaning of loving God with ALL your heart, soul, and might? Why is this important for us to know and understand?** (Encourage a few responses.)

SUMMARY

God wants His people to rightly fear Him. He is the one true God and is worthy of our highest honor and respect. We show a right fear of God by obeying His commands. God's commands are meant to lead us to our greatest treasure and reward—God Himself. That is why the most important command is to love God most of all. God knows we cannot be truly happy apart from knowing, honoring, and loving Him. Loving God means experiencing and treating God as your greatest treasure and joy. Loving God is having wholehearted devotion to Him—loving Him more than food, activities, pets, friends, and even family. Loving God is seeking after Him as your greatest passion, wanting to follow Him because there is nothing or no one else who can satisfy you and bring you true, lasting happiness.

07

ENGAGE THE
HEART

Choose one or more of the following topics to discuss.

GOD DESIRES A RELATIONSHIP WITH MAN

When God came down to meet with the people of Israel on Mount Sinai, He committed Himself to a relationship with them (Exodus 19:5). Was this because of some deficiency in God (God was lonely and needed friends)**? How do you know this is not the case? (See Acts 17:25.) Why do we want relationships with others? Does God have the same needs as we do? Why then does He desire a relationship with man?**

You may want to look at Ephesians 1:4-6 for help in answering this question. The main point that your child needs to understand is that God loves from the overflow of His love. He chooses to love people because He is loving. Man was created to be the receiver of God's gracious love and care.

What does this tell you about God?

PROVEN LOVE AND FAITHFULNESS

God did not just give Israel His law and commands and ask for blind obedience. He first proved His love, faithfulness, and goodness. **What did He do to show His character to Israel?** God has also shown each of us His love, goodness, and faithfulness. **What examples of this do you have from your own life? How should this influence or affect your love for God and your trust in God?**

LOVING GOD

Does loving the LORD with "all your heart and with all your soul and with all your might" sound difficult? Why? What pulls your heart away from God? What attitudes do you need to address? What thoughts make dull (lessen) your love for God? What actions will help you to love God more? Can you do this on your own? Why is love for God a gift? If it is a gift, why then must we fight to love God more (why are our efforts needed)? Is loving God just a feeling?

> **Loving God means experiencing and treating God as your greatest treasure and joy.**

Make sure that your child understands that loving God is more than mere emotion. It is a commitment and a decision that we make, and a desire that we nurture. To help your child to understand this you may want to ask him what loving another person looks like (e.g., being concerned about that person, thinking about and doing what would make the other person happy, spending time with that person, talking about the person in positive ways, standing up for that person). Then ask what a greater love for God looks like.

GAZING UPON THE BEAUTY OF THE LORD

What does it mean to "gaze upon the beauty of the LORD?" How can you gaze upon the beauty of the LORD? What in your life keeps you from meditating (considering, pondering, letting your mind dwell, careful thought, fixing your attention on) the Lord? What distractions can you lessen or remove? What kind of accountability would be helpful to you?

DUTY AND DELIGHT

What is the difference between **duty** (what you should do) **and delight** (what you enjoy)? **Is it wrong to do things from duty? How can what is a duty be turned to a delight? What thoughts, emotions, decisions, longings, truths, and graces do you think led the psalmist to his desire expressed in Psalm 42:1-2?**

07

> *As a deer pants for flowing streams, so pants my soul for you, O God. ²My soul thirsts for God, for the living God.*—PSALM 42:1-2A

How is this helpful for you to think about?

THE THINGS OF EARTH

In Psalm 73:25-26, the psalmist says, "there is nothing on earth I desire besides you." **What are some of the things on earth that you desire? Do they interfere with your longing for God? How? Do you want to desire God above all else? Is this something you often pray for? How can you make it a regular prayer of yours?**

INFLUENCE THE WILL

What action or actions can you take this week that will encourage you to treasure God most?

FAMILY WORSHIP TIME

Read the words of the hymn, "Take My Life and Let It Be" by Frances R. Havergal (*Hymns of Grace*, 393, or find it on the internet.) **How does the hymn writer convey a sense of the desire to love God most of all? How could you apply some of these to your own life?** Sing the hymn together.

God's laws and commands are

**HOLY,
RIGHTEOUS,
AND GOOD**

because they have
been shaped
by God's character.

GOD CALLS HIS PEOPLE TO BE HOLY

INTRODUCTION FOR PARENTS

Of all the attributes of God, the one that most encompasses the entirety of His divine essence is His holiness. God's holiness is, in a sense, His "God-ness"—signifying everything about Him that separates Him from everything else in creation. God is like nothing else. The triune God is completely and utterly unique, beyond comparison! Because God is holy, we as His image bearers must be holy in the manner in which we regard Him. We must treat Him with the honor, respect, reverence, trust, love, and devotion that He truly deserves, at all times.

God's holiness also describes His moral perfection and His separateness from all sin. Therefore, in order to live in joyful fellowship with Him forever, we are required to exhibit this moral perfection, too. How do we know what this moral perfection consists of? How do we ascertain what is holy conduct in God's eyes? By looking to God's holy and righteous law and commands. Yes, commands.[1]

Here is a very timely and thoughtful word from Pastor Kevin DeYoung:

> It sounds very spiritual to say God is interested in a relationship, not in rules. But it's not biblical. From top to bottom, the Bible is full of commands.

[1] Nelson, Jill. *To Be Like Jesus: A Study for Children on Following Jesus* Teacher's Guide. (Minneapolis, Minn.: Truth78, 2017), 11.

They aren't meant to stifle a relationship with God, but to protect it, seal it, and define it.[2]

This is a concept that is often minimized when teaching children. However, it is crucial for giving shape, context, and understanding of the Gospel. Therefore, think of this devotion as a means of pointing forward, setting a foundation for our desperate need for a perfect, law-keeping Savior.

08

> **GATHER:** Dinner or paper plate, garbage or waste materials, desirable treat

PIQUE THEIR INTEREST

OPTION 1—Before you sit down to do this devotion, take a DINNER PLATE (or PAPER PLATE) and fill it with GARBAGE and/or other WASTE MATERIALS. Then, place a DESIRABLE TREAT in the GARBAGE, covering it somewhat.

> Suppose I promised a special treat for you today and gave it to you like this. (Display the plate.) Would you find anything wrong with this? What? Would you want to eat the treat? Why not?

OPTION 2—Pose the same scenario, as follows:

> Suppose I promised you a special treat for you today like your favorite type of (donut, candy, etc.), but I gave it to you on a plate covered in trash—used tissues, muddy rags, and old rotted food. Would you want to eat the treat? Why not?

Give a short summary of the illustration.

> Special things are meant to be treated in a certain way. They should be "set apart" and not be mixed with worthless, icky things. This would be wrong. A person would be right to say, "No, I will not eat this. It has been spoiled."

---

[2]DeYoung, Kevin. *The Hole in Our Holiness: Filling the Gap between Gospel Passion and the Pursuit of Godliness.* (Wheaton, Ill.: Crossway, 2012), 45.

INSTRUCT THE
MIND

Introduce, read, and interact with the following Scriptures.

As we have seen in the previous devotions, in the Old Testament, God chose Israel to be His treasured possession. As God's chosen people, they had special privileges: They would experience God's special love, care, guidance, and protection. But, as God's chosen people, they also had special responsibilities. They were to look and act in certain ways—ways that would reflect and show that they were God's treasured people.

08

> *"For I am the LORD your God. Consecrate*
> *yourselves therefore, and be holy, for I am holy...*
> *⁴⁵ For I am the LORD who brought you up out of the*
> *land of Egypt to be your God. You shall therefore*
> *be holy, for I am holy."*—LEVITICUS 11:44-45

What is God calling His people "to be" in these verses? [holy] **Why does He call His people to be holy?** [because He is holy] **What does it mean to "be holy"?** (Encourage a few responses. For younger children, give them a hint. To be holy would be like the opposite of the plate full of garbage—a clean, spotless plate.)

Because God is holy, He is perfectly pure and separate from everything wrong and sinful. That God is holy also means that He always acts in ways that show that He alone is God and is perfect in every way. It means that God always thinks, says, and does what is right.

For God's people to be holy means to be "consecrated" or set apart by being completely devoted to God, treating Him with the honor and love He deserves at all times. It means always doing what is right in His sight—in every thought, desire, word, and action. God's treasured possession is not to be like our special treat placed among garbage and trash. Just as you would be disgusted by a treat spoiled by trash, even more so, a holy God cannot tolerate (accept) His people being tainted (polluted, contaminated) and spoiled by sin.

This is what the prophet Habakkuk said about God:

> *"You who are of purer eyes than to see evil*
> *and cannot look at wrong,"*—HABAKKUK 1:13A

So, how were God's people to know what is holy and right conduct (behavior)—holy and right thoughts, desires, words, and actions? (Encourage a few responses.)

Here is what God had Moses say to the people of Israel:

> *"And now, Israel, what does the LORD your God*
> *require of you, but to fear the LORD your God, to*
> *walk in all his ways, to love him, to serve the LORD*
> *your God with all your heart and with all your soul,*
> *¹³and to keep the commandments and statutes*
> *of the LORD, which I am commanding you today*
> *for your good?"*—DEUTERONOMY 10:12-13

Moses says that God "requires" something from His people. **What is a requirement?** [something that you must do; it's not optional; not something you do if you feel like it but don't have to do] **What are the first four requirements listed?** [fear the LORD, walk in His ways, love Him, serve Him] **How would people know if they are doing these in the right way?** Look at verse 13. **What was Israel "to keep"?** [the commandments and statutes, or rules, of the LORD]

Here is what the apostle Paul said about God's law and commands in the New Testament:

> *So the law is holy, and the commandment is*
> *holy and righteous and good.*—ROMANS 7:12

SUMMARY

In order "to be" holy, God's people are required "to keep" His commandments. All of these commands were given so that God's people would know what kind of conduct—what thoughts, feelings, words, and actions are holy and right. God's laws and commands are holy and righteous because they have been shaped by God's character. They show His perfect nature and moral purity. They show His goodness and wise ways. They show His love and protection for His people. These commands show what is pleasing and acceptable to a holy God. God requires what is best and greatest. God cannot tolerate anything less. It wouldn't be right for God to say "okay" to any kind of unholy conduct because He Himself is holy. A special

> **A special treat is unacceptable when mixed with garbage. In a similar way, God cannot look with approval on unholy people.**

08

treat is unacceptable when mixed with garbage. In a similar way, God cannot look with approval on unholy people.

But these holy and righteous commands were not given just to the people of Israel. Even now God calls His chosen people to be holy and righteous. It is the only way to truly glorify God. Being perfectly righteous and holy is absolutely necessary for enjoying eternal life with God (Hebrews 12:14). That means you and I must be holy, too, if we are to enjoy eternal life with God. This should cause all of us to think very seriously about our thoughts, feelings, words, and actions. Do you really please God at all times? Do you always keep His holy, righteous, and good commands? Do you think that you can please God simply by working harder to obey Him? These are all important questions. In the next several devotions, we will see how the Bible answers these questions.

ENGAGE THE HEART

Choose one or more of the following topics to discuss.

PRIVILEGE AND RESPONSIBILITY

Just like Israel, all Christians have special privileges. Along with those privileges comes responsibilities. **Can you think of a practical example in real life where privileges and responsibilities are linked?** [e.g., getting a driving license is linked to driving responsibly and taking care of the car; having the privilege of staying up later is linked to the responsibility of getting up on time the next day] **Why are privilege and responsibility linked in the Christian life?** (Make sure your child understands that being in a special covenant relationship with God also means accepting the responsibility of living in obedience to Him.) **How is this demonstrated in earthly relationships?** [e.g., having the benefits of being part of a family also means that you make contributions to the family, such as encouraging each other, helping a sibling with homework, performing household chores] **Is it unfair or unkind to expect commitment to each other in a relationship? Why not?**

SET APART

Give some practical examples of being set apart by being completely devoted to God, treating Him with the honor and love He deserves, at all times.

In what ways was Israel set apart from the other nations? How does this apply today? Are there any ways in which you need to grow in being set apart?

PURE

Habakkuk says of God, *"You who are of purer eyes than to see evil and cannot look at wrong."*—HABAKKUK 1:13 Since God's children are to be a reflection of who He is, what does this say about who we should be? What is your reaction to things that are evil or wrong? (Try to help your child to determine if he has a holy distaste for those things that are inappropriate, or if he has a tolerance or even a desire for them.) Are there things that you view, read, think, or participate in that contaminate your purity? What changes do you need to make? How can you make them?

THE GOODNESS OF GOD'S WAYS

In Deuteronomy 6:1-3, God tells Israel (and us) to *"fear the LORD your God…by keeping all his statutes and his commandments… that it may go well with you."* Give some practical examples of how keeping God's commands are good for you. Give some practical examples of how ignoring God's commands is destructive. **How should this influence your attitude toward obeying God? What does this warning in Deuteronomy tell you about God's love?**

KEEPING THE LAW

Romans 7:12 tells us that God's commands are *"holy and righteous and good."* **Do you really believe that—that being generous is better than being selfish, that being kind is better than being mean, that "seeking things that are above" is better than loving the world? Does your life reflect that you believe God's ways are best? What prevents you from obeying the law? Why is it that what we say we believe so often does not match the way we live? What does this show you about your need for Christ and your need to depend on God?** Explain.

08

INFLUENCE THE
WILL

What action or actions can you take this week to understand the holiness of God better and to discover what it means to be a "set apart" people? What can you do practically, or what changes do you need to make to appreciate and walk in purity?

FAMILY WORSHIP TIME

Hum the tune to the hymn "Holy, Holy, Holy" by Reginald Heber (*Hymns of Grace*, 48, or find it on the internet), and see if your family can guess the name of the hymn. Then read the words, defining any words or phrases that are unfamiliar. **How do the words convey a sense of the holiness of God and a right response to His holiness? How does the tune help communicate a sense of serious reverence for God?** Sing the hymn together.

Apart from understanding the bad news of how **DESPERATELY SINFUL** *you are, you will never truly love the good news of the Gospel.*

ALL HAVE SINNED

INTRODUCTION FOR PARENTS

In his excellent book, *What Is the Gospel?*, Greg Gilbert relates the story of getting a speeding ticket. He took the ticket, checked the box that acknowledged, "I plead guilty to the charge," and then mailed in a check for the $35 fine. He comments,

> I'm a convicted criminal. For some reason, though, even though I checked the guilty box, I don't feel terribly guilty. I'm not going to lose any sleep over my walk on the wrong side of the law.[1]

He shares this story in order to illustrate how we tend to have this same demeanor in relation to the guilt of our sin. And we are especially prone to convey this kind of casualness to our children and youth. The essence, depth, and gravity of sin is often minimized in order to quickly jump to the good news of the Gospel. But consider these words from John Piper:

> Sin is not an innocent mistake or a funny blunder or a noble flaw. Sin is ugly rebellion against God. Paul calls this sinful generation "a crooked and perverse generation" (Philippians 2:15). The Bible uses words like "abomination," and Paul describes fallen man in Romans 3:13, "Their throat is an open grave;

[1] Gilbert, Gregory D. *What Is the Gospel?* (Wheaton, Ill.: Crossway, 2010), 48.

they use their tongues to deceive. The venom of asps is under their lips." Sin is abhorrent and ugly.

If our children are ever to grasp the gospel, they must grasp this about themselves. And we parents must! They and we are sinful—dreadfully sinful. Until this is seen and felt in some significant measure, the gospel will not be cherished.[2]

In this devotion, we want to acquaint our children with the ugliness of sin and the desperate condition of sinners. We want them to see sin as God does—as treason against our holy, sovereign Creator. We also want them to ponder seriously God's righteous condemnation of sinners—His eternal wrath. While these are hard truths to teach, they are essential truths meant to deepen our amazement, love, and worship of the one and only Savior, Jesus.

09

PIQUE THEIR INTEREST

Pose the following scenario:

Suppose you told me you were so hungry that you could eat 10 large pizzas. **Is there a way I could show you that you couldn't do this?** [give you 10 pizzas, showing that it would be too much food for your stomach to hold]

Or suppose I saw that there was a bright pink spot on your forehead but you didn't believe me. **Is there something I could do to show this to be true—something that would help you to see the spot?** [hand you a mirror so that you could see the spot on your face]

What if someone had a spot on his forehead but it wasn't simply a spot of pink paint. **What if it was cancer? Why would it be really important for me to show that person the spot?**

These pretend scenarios make an important point: There are ways to show us the truth about the way things really are. And knowing the truth about something can be really important—so important that it could mean the difference between life and death.

---

[2]Piper, John. "Help the Children Love the Different People," sermon delivered at Bethlehem Baptist Church of Minneapolis, Minn. on January 17, 2010, copyright Desiring God Foundation, desiringGod.org.

INSTRUCT THE
MIND

Introduce, read, and interact with the following Scriptures.

In our last devotion, we learned that God had called His chosen people, Israel, to be holy because God is holy. Israel was to be set apart from the other nations. The people of Israel were to be completely devoted to God by fearing, loving, serving, and obeying Him—worshiping God alone. All of their thoughts, feelings, words, and actions were to be pleasing to God. God gave His people His laws and commands to show them what kind of behavior was holy and righteous. However, the law serves another purpose. Just as a mirror acts to show you a spot on your forehead, God's commands act like a kind of mirror, too—showing something very important.

09

> as it is written: "None is righteous, no, not one;
> ¹¹no one understands; no one seeks for God.
> ¹²All have turned aside; together they have become
> worthless; no one does good, not even one."
> ¹³"Their throat is an open grave; they use their
> tongues to deceive." "The venom of asps is under
> their lips." ¹⁴"Their mouth is full of curses and
> bitterness." ¹⁵"Their feet are swift to shed blood;
> ¹⁶in their paths are ruin and misery, ¹⁷and the
> way of peace they have not known." ¹⁸"There is no
> fear of God before their eyes."—ROMANS 3:10-18

In these verses, the apostle Paul is quoting several texts from the Old Testament. These verses describe not only the people of Israel, but all people.

How would you summarize what these verses are telling us? (Encourage a few responses.) **Can you give a few examples from the Old Testament that show this to be true?** [Give a few examples of people or events: the wicked people during the time of Noah, Pharaoh and the Egyptians, Israel made and worshipped a golden calf, David sinned with Bathsheba and had Uriah killed, Israel rejected God and demanded a king, etc.]

Now listen carefully to what verse 20 says,

> *For by works of the law no human being will*
> *be justified in his sight, since through the law*
> *comes knowledge of sin.*—ROMANS 3:20

What do we come to know through God's law and commands? [a knowledge of sin; we see that we are sinners]

In a way, God's law and commands act like a mirror—a kind of mirror showing us our sin, showing us our true condition. I might think to myself, "I'm good and do what is right so God will accept and approve of me," but God's commands would show me that this is not true.

09

What does it mean to be "justified" in God's sight? [to be judged holy and righteous by God, to be pleasing in His sight, etc.] **So, when Paul says, "For by works of the law no human being will be justified," what does he mean? Can someone be acceptable to God by keeping the law? Will God say to you, "You have done a good job of obeying, so now you can enjoy eternal life with Me."?** [no]

A few verses later Paul says this:

> *for all have sinned and fall short of*
> *the glory of God,*—ROMANS 3:23

This includes you and me; it includes all people in all places, of all ages. We all fall short of glorifying God—we all fail to glorify God. We fail because we don't fear Him as we should, love Him as we should, serve Him as we should, or obey Him as we should. God's holy and righteous commands show us—prove to us—that we are sinners.

Why is this important for you and me to know? Why should you care about these truths? (Encourage a few responses.)

Here are a few verses explaining why this is a life or death matter...

> *For the wages of sin is death,*—ROMANS 6:23A

> *...the wrath of God comes upon the sons*
> *of disobedience.*—EPHESIANS 5:6B

> *They will suffer the punishment of eternal*
> *destruction, away from the presence of*
> *the Lord...*—2 THESSALONIANS 1:9A

SUMMARY

God's law is holy, righteous, and good because it has been shaped by God's own character. It is meant to guide God's people in what is pleasing to God. But God's law and commands also show us something very important and very sad. They show us our true heart condition. They prove to us that we are sinners who have repeatedly rebelled against our Creator. We show our sinful nature every single time we break one of God's perfect commands. A quick lie. Complaining in our hearts. A little envy. Being more excited by a sporting event than by God. Every sin is ugly, terrible, and offensive to God. It is like shaking your fist at God and saying to Him, "You are not that great! I don't need to do what You say. I can do what I want. I don't need You to be happy!"

> We show our sinful nature every single time we break one of God's perfect commands... Every sin is ugly, terrible, and offensive to God. It is like shaking your fist at God and saying to Him, "You are not that great! I don't need to do what You say. I can do what I want. I don't need You to be happy!"

09

But the truth is, God is greater than all. He is the one true God who created us and rules over us. He decides what is true and right and good. God is holy, He cannot ignore our sin and pretend like it doesn't matter. It matters a lot. In fact, God's response to our sin is our greatest problem. God is filled with righteous anger—wrath—toward sin. Sin deserves the most severe punishment imaginable—experiencing God's anger forever in hell. No amount of trying harder to obey God's commands will solve that problem. We are completely helpless. Eternal life and lasting joy with God cannot be earned by any of our own efforts or hard work.

Why is this so important to know and understand? Because until you know your true problem and how desperate you are, you will not seek after the right solution. You will not see how much you need a Savior. You will not see what Jesus came to save you from and what He saves you for. Apart from understanding the bad news of how desperately sinful you are, you will never truly love the good news of the Gospel.

ENGAGE THE HEART

Choose one or more of the following topics to discuss:

NO ONE SEEKS GOD

09

Romans 3:11 says that no one seeks God. **What does this mean?**

Make sure your child understands that, in our sinful state, we have no desire or ability to seek God. We, by nature reject, God. We are helpless and lost.

Does this mean that God cannot be found? Explain.

Make sure your child understands that since there is nothing in us that desires a relationship with

> **In His mercy and grace, God has given us His Word to show us who He is...and our need. God gives man the heart to seek Him... and the means to know Him.**

God, the only hope we have is that God reaches down to man. God initiates the drawing of our hearts to Him. Without God's initiation, we have no hope. In His mercy and grace, God has given us His Word to show us who He is...and our need. God gives man the heart to seek Him...and the means to know Him.

NO ONE DOES GOOD

Does Romans 3:12 sound like an overstatement—that *"no one does good, not even one"*? Can you think of examples of people who have done good? Since we know that the Bible is true in all its parts, how can this verse be true?

Make sure your child understands that "the good" that man does is often contaminated by impure motives—pride, self-centeredness, fear of man, etc. There is no "pure good" that man does. Though a person may perform an act of goodness, by nature man is sinful at heart and so even our good acts are self-serving. Only a heart transformation of our sin nature can result in us doing good—even though the good that Christians do still is not pure goodness. It may be less contaminated by sinful motives, but there are always conflicting motives in our hearts— some pure and some impure. It is impossible for us to do anything completely void of sin. You may want to look at Hebrews 11:6a to show your child that *"without faith it is impossible to please* [God].*"* So anything done apart from faith in Christ falls short of pleasing God.

What are some "good" things you have done? Think very carefully. **What are the pure and impure motives behind that good action? Can you say you did it in total purity?**

Can you ever do enough "good" to be acceptable to God?

Help your child to understand that our good works do not make us right with God. Since we all fail to achieve (reach) God's standards of righteousness, we must be made righteous through faith.

09

THE SINFUL TONGUE

Romans 3:13 and 14 continue to comment on our speech—*"they use their tongues to deceive." "The venom of asps is under their lips." "Their mouth is full of curses and bitterness."*

Can you give some examples of this kind of speech? Have you ever had this kind of speech come out of your mouth? What is in the heart when this kind of speech comes out of the mouth? How does this prove to us that our sin nature is real?

THINKING HIGHLY OF OURSELVES

Many people think that the key to being happy is having something called a "high self-esteem." By this they mean that you should think good thoughts about yourself. You should remind yourself how special you are, and focus on other "positive" thoughts. **What is wrong with this thinking? According to the Bible, will this kind of thinking make you truly happy? Why not?** (Be sure your child understands that we were not created to be made much of, but to make much of God.[3]) **Why is it loving to help another person understand his sinful state outside of Christ (without trusting in Jesus' payment for his unrighteousness)?**

....
[3]See Isaiah 43:7, Jeremiah 9:23-24, and 2 Corinthians 10:17.

SINFUL ACTIONS

Romans 3:15 continues with these words, *"Their feet are swift to shed blood; in their paths are ruin and misery, and the way of peace they have not known."*

These verses are talking about the sinful actions of sinful man. Though you may not have "shed blood" (killed anyone), there are many ways in which we hurt one another. **Can you name some of them? What is the motivation** (the heart attitudes) **behind these actions? Do you see any of this sin in yourself?**

WORKS OF THE LAW DO NOT JUSTIFY

09

Can you see now why *"by works of the law no human will be justified"* **in the sight of God** (Romans 3:20)? **Why? Are you justified by your works, speech, thoughts, and attitudes? In what ways do you fall short or fail to keep the law?** (If you have not discussed Hebrews 11:6a, bring in the truth that without faith we cannot please God. We are not justified by our works, but by faith in Christ.)

How does the sin of man show that they do not fear God? *"There is no fear of God before their eyes."*—ROMANS 3:18 **What becomes more important to sinful man than fearing God?** (Make sure that your child understands that our sin nature causes us to love our sin more than we fear the wrath of God. We are blind to our true nature and our own condition.)

It is easy for people growing up in Christian homes and the church to think of themselves as good. When they compare themselves to others, they see that they are not like others who are more sinful than they are. **Have you ever done this?** Give an example. **Does "being better" than someone else mean that we are justified** (judged holy and righteous) **before God? What is the true standard that we should measure ourselves against?** [God's holiness] **What does this do to our boasting?**

THE WRATH OF GOD AND PUNISHMENT

The Bible says, the "wrath of God comes upon the sons of disobedience" (Ephesians 5:6b) and "the wages of sin is death"

(Romans 6:23a). Explain these verses. **Do you live with this sense of the seriousness of sin?** Explain. **If not, why not?** (Our eyes are blinded to the seriousness of sin. What blinds our eyes and hearts?) [pride, an unwillingness to examine our hearts, repeated sin becomes commonplace to us and we become comfortable with it, we don't believe that God would really punish sin, we see God as only loving, etc.] **How can you recover a sense of the seriousness of sin?**

INFLUENCE THE
WILL

09

What action or actions can you take this week to see the seriousness of your sin and to examine your heart to see the conflicting motives in the "good" that you do? Ask God to give you a heart of repentance.

FAMILY WORSHIP TIME

Read the first verse but not the chorus of the hymn, "All I Have Is Christ" by Jordan Kauflin (*Hymns of Grace*, 389, or find it on the internet). **What does the writer want us to understand about the condition of his heart and life? Why is this important to understand?** Now read the chorus and the rest of the hymn. **What changed in his life?** Sing the hymn together.

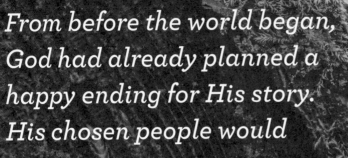

From before the world began, God had already planned a happy ending for His story. His chosen people would

LIVE WITH HIM

and enjoy His fellowship forever. But it would involve a final solution to the problem of sin.

10

GOD'S GRACIOUS REDEMPTIVE PLAN

INTRODUCTION FOR PARENTS

Hopefully, the previous devotion served to encourage a serious and sober reflection of the depth, gravity, and problem of our sin before a holy God. This is not a popular concept in our day. We would rather simply tell our children about God's love and mercy as seen in the Person and work of Christ. But the late Jerry Bridges offers a critical reminder:

> The love of God has no meaning apart from Calvary. And Calvary has no meaning apart from the holy and just wrath of God. Jesus did not die just to give us peace and a purpose in life; He died to save us from the wrath of God. He died to reconcile us to a holy God who was alienated from us because of our sin. He died to ransom us from the penalty of sin—the punishment of everlasting destruction, shut out from the presence of the Lord. He died that we, the just objects of God's wrath, should become, by His grace, heirs of God and co-heirs with Him. [1]

In this devotion, we are going to provide a very brief overview of some key themes in redemptive history in which God's holiness, judgment, love, and mercy are demonstrated so that children and youth will better understand the progressive revelation of God's glorious salvation, which then comes to completion in the Person and work of Christ.

....
[1] Bridges, Jerry. *The Practice of Godliness: Godliness Has Value for All Things.* (Carol Stream, Ill.: NavPress, 1983), 24.

PIQUE THEIR INTEREST

Pose the following scenario:

> Suppose I told you that I had just read a really exciting adventure story, and I wanted to share it with you. So, I read to you the last few sentences of the story which said,
>
> "And when he finally entered the city, all the people rejoiced because of the amazing deeds he had done in defeating Halak. Day after day, the people gathered together and listened as he told them of his many adventures in the far off lands of Plator."
>
> **Would those sentences provide you with enough information about what actually happened in the story? What more would you need to know?** [Possible responses: Who is the hero? What's his name? What did he do? Who is Halak, and why was he/she/it an enemy?]
>
> Stories need context if we are going to understand them. We need to know the beginning of the story and read about the main characters, the problems they encounter along the way, and how those problems are solved. We can't really appreciate the happy ending unless we know what came before.

10

INSTRUCT THE MIND

Introduce, read, and interact with the following Scriptures:

> In a way, the Bible can be understood as a story, too. It is a story telling us about the most important things that have ever happened in the past, what we are experiencing now, and what will happen in the future. It is a true story because it is authored by God Himself. And just as in our pretend story, it's important for us to know not just the end, but the beginning and everything in between so that we see how everything fits together.

In our last devotion, we talked about the problem of our sin and a holy God's fierce anger at sin—His wrath. Because all of us sin, we all deserve God's punishment of death and hell. We are now experiencing life in a broken world under the curse of sin. But that's not the end of the story, nor is it the beginning.

The Bible begins with God creating everything and pronouncing it "good." After creating man and woman in His image and likeness for His glory, God pronounced the seventh day "very good." So, what happened? How did we all end up as sinners deserving God's judgment?

> *...sin came into the world through one man,*
> *and death through sin, and so death spread*
> *to all men because all sinned*—ROMANS 5:12B

10

Who is the "one man" in this verse? [Adam] **How did Adam and Eve sin against God?** [by listening to the serpent instead of to God and eating from the one tree that God had commanded them not to eat from; by rejecting God's rule over them] **What had God promised if they were to eat from the one tree?** [They would die.] Remember: *"the wages of sin is death"* (Romans 6:23a). **What does this show about God's character?** [God is holy and will not tolerate or ignore sin. God is faithful and keeps His Word.] **But did they die right away?** [no] **Why not? What does this tell us about God's character?** [He is loving, patient, merciful, etc.]

God did pronounce judgment on them: They would have to leave the garden, and their lives and the rest of the world would experience the terrible effects of sin. And yes, they would also die. But God also did something very amazing. He made a promise and gave a provision.

> [God said to the serpent,] *"I will put enmity*
> *between you and the woman, and between your*
> *offspring and her offspring; he shall bruise your*
> *head, and you shall bruise his heel."*
> —GENESIS 3:15

This verse contains a hopeful promise about something that will happen to the serpent—Satan. What is it? [Something will happen to the serpent's "head." Satan's head will be "bruised" or crushed by one of Eve's descendants—a man.]

*And the LORD God made for Adam and for his wife
garments of skins and clothed them.*—GENESIS 3:21

What provision did God make (what did God provide for) **Adam
and Eve?** [garments of skins] **What are garments of "skins"?** [the
skins of animals] **For that to happen, what did God first have to
do to the animals, and why is this important?** [The animals had to
be killed first. The penalty of sin is death. Something had to die.]

*...without the shedding of blood there is no
forgiveness of sins.*—HEBREWS 9:22B

This provision was a sad reminder to Adam and Eve (and all of
us) of the tragic and deadly consequences of sin. God could not
look upon their sin and just pretend it wasn't there. So God, in His
love and mercy, provided a way that His sinful people could be
forgiven. But for God to be righteous and just, something had to
die—blood had to be shed. God provided a substitute, the blood of
animals. This was an undeserved kindness from God given to His
sinful people. That is what mercy is.

*But you, O Lord, are a God merciful and
gracious, slow to anger and abounding in
steadfast love and faithfulness.*—PSALM 86:15

Throughout the sad storyline of the Old Testament, there are
wonderful glimpses of God's merciful and gracious promise
and provision. For example, God gave Israel special priests
who would act as go-betweens between Himself and the sinful
people. God gave these priests exact instructions for sacrifices.
These sacrifices, done in the right way with the right heart
attitude, would allow God's people to live in fellowship with Him.
Over and over, and over again, thousands upon thousands of
animals were killed. The people kept sinning, so new sacrifices
were needed. That is because the blood of animals wasn't enough
to truly solve the real problem.

*...it can never, by the same sacrifices that are
continually offered every year, make perfect
those who draw near. ²Otherwise, would they not
have ceased to be offered, since the worshipers,
having once been cleansed, would no longer*

10

have any consciousness of sins? ³But in these sacrifices there is a reminder of sins every year. ⁴For it is impossible for the blood of bulls and goats to take away sins.—HEBREWS 10:1B-4

What could these sacrifices not do? [give you a clean conscience, because they could not take away sin]

This was no surprise to God. God knew the killing of animals could never take away sin—it could only cover it up, like throwing a nice clean blanket over a pile of dirty, stinky garbage. These animal sacrifices were a temporary solution, and were a loving, merciful, and gracious provision of God for His people. A better and final solution was promised.

> God knew the killing of animals could never take away sin—it could only cover it up, like throwing a nice, clean blanket over a pile of dirty, stinky garbage. These animal sacrifices were a temporary solution, and were a loving, merciful, and gracious provision of God for His people.

10

A High Priest would come and offer a perfect sacrifice. For hundreds and hundreds of years of Old Testament history, God's people waited and waited and waited. Then one day, a man named John saw a man approaching him and said,

"Behold, the Lamb of God, who takes away the sin of the world!"—JOHN 1:29B

Who is the Lamb of God? [Jesus]

SUMMARY

The Bible has a storyline that we need to see and understand. In the beginning, we read of God creating, for His glory, Adam and Eve who then rebel against God and sin. We see God judging Satan, Adam and Eve, and their future descendants. As we continue reading through the Old Testament, we see time and time again the terrible consequences of sin—ruin, misery, death, and destruction. Nothing is left untouched. Sin is terrible. It changes everything.

However, God is sovereign over this story. From all eternity—from before the world began, God had already planned a happy ending for His story. His chosen people would live with Him and enjoy His fellowship forever. But it would involve a final solution to the problem of sin. A final Priest would

> We see time and time again the terrible consequences of sin—ruin, misery, death, and destruction. Nothing is left untouched. Sin is terrible. It changes everything.

come and offer a final sacrifice that would take away sin once and for all, and not just cover it up. The Hero of the story would arrive and do what Adam and God's people failed to do. His name is Jesus. Jesus the High Priest. Jesus the Lamb of God. Jesus the Savior. Jesus the King of kings.

10

ENGAGE THE
HEART

Choose one or more of the following topics to discuss:

A BROKEN WORLD

What are some of the effects of the Fall that you see in the world and in your own family? Describe what the world would be like without this brokenness. **What does God's original design for creation tell you about the heart of God?**

SIN THROUGH ONE MAN

Do you think it is fair that sin came into the world through one man? Explain. Adam and Eve were free to choose to obey God or disobey, and both of them chose to rebel against God. (Two out of two persons chose rebellion.) **Do you think it would be any different if you had been the one in the Garden?**

Does anyone make you sin when you sin, or is it a choice you make? Are you responsible for your choices even though you have a sin nature inherited from Adam?

Is it "fair" that redemption should come through one Man? Explain.

Make sure your children understand that if they think it is unfair to inherit a sin nature from Adam that it would follow then that it is unfair that salvation should be offered through one man.

Do we deserve the mercy that God shows man through the cross? Does God owe sinners forgiveness? Why not?

Help your children to see that their sin condemns them, and they have no right to have someone take their place and absorb the wrath of God against sin—any more than they would have the right to have someone else's perfect score on a test that they failed.

JUDGMENT AND MERCY

10

What does this chapter show you about the reality of God's judgment? Some people say that God would never punish anyone in hell. Is this true? How do you know this? Why is God right to punish sin? (Why can't He pretend that sin does not matter, or that it does not exist?) What would happen if there were no punishment for sin and evil?

> God is slow to anger and abounding in steadfast love and faithfulness.

Why was it merciful of God to provide the blood of animals to forgive sin in Old Testament times? What other evidences do you see of God's mercy in the Bible, in the world today and in your life? Does God have to be merciful to anyone? (In a sense, this is a trick question because man does not deserve mercy. However, God's character is merciful and inclines Him to show kindness to sinners.) Does this mean that God must be patient with man forever and withhold judgment? Why not? Explain. Why is this important? [God's mercy is not to be taken for granted, nor is it unlimited toward unrepentant sinners. This should encourage us to repent of our sin and trust in Jesus for salvation.]

REMINDERS OF SIN

The constant need to sacrifice animals to forgive sin was a continual reminder to the Israelites of their sin. We do not have this reminder today. **Are you aware daily of your sin? How did you sin today? Did you think about this before now? What makes it easy to ignore or minimize** (make it seem less important) **our sin? How can you be conscious of your sin and the need to repent?** (What practical steps can you take to examine your heart and trust in the sacrifice of Jesus?)

THE LAMB OF GOD

Why is the provision of a permanent sacrifice for sin such good news? What does this tell you about God? When you grow up hearing the Gospel message over and over, is it easy to take it for granted—to not realize just what glorious news it is? **What are indications** (signs) **of taking the Gospel for granted? How can you gain a greater appreciation for the Gospel?** (Think of some practical practices that will help influence your heart.)

10

INFLUENCE THE WILL

What action or actions can you take to appreciate the good news of the Gospel and to share it with others?

FAMILY WORSHIP TIME

Read the words of the hymn, "Grace Greater Than Our Sin" by Julia H. Johnston (*Hymns of Grace*, 78, or find it on the internet). Define unfamiliar words and see if your children can identify words and phrases that point to man's sin and God's wrath, love, and mercy. **What does the hymn writer hold up as the centerpiece of God's mercy? Why is this important for us to know?**

PRAYER TIME

Write a prayer for your children. Pray that they will understand the gravity of their sin, recognize Jesus as the hero of their story, and accept God's gift of mercy.

10

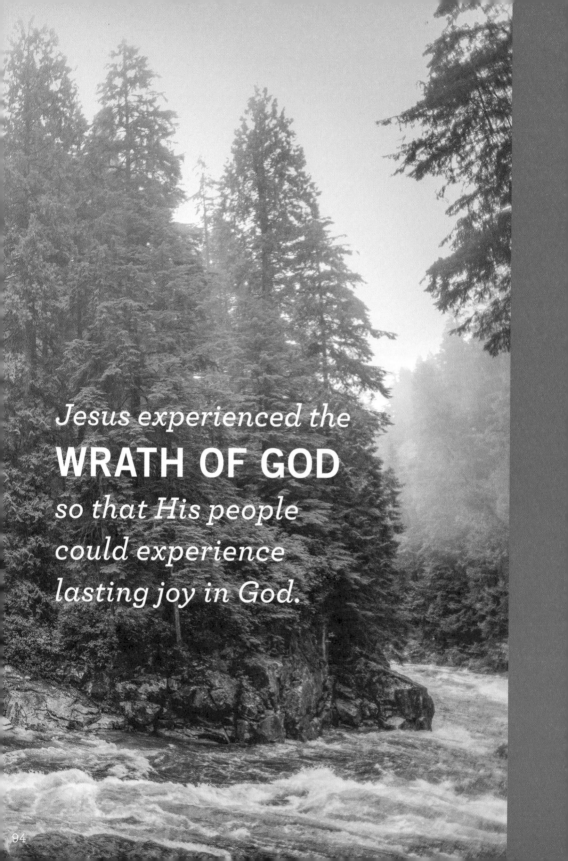

Jesus experienced the **WRATH OF GOD** *so that His people could experience lasting joy in God.*

JESUS, THE ONLY SAVIOR

INTRODUCTION FOR PARENTS

Parents, how do you think your child would answer these questions?

> Why is it important that Jesus never sinned?
>
> Why did Jesus die on the cross?
>
> What did Jesus experience on the cross? Why is this important to know?
>
> What does Jesus' resurrection prove?

Why are these questions important to ask? Because our children need to see and understand the importance of Jesus' perfect life, death on the cross, and resurrection so that they may comprehend justification. Justification is at the core of understanding the Gospel. It is why the Reformation that Martin Luther sparked more than 500 years ago is still important for us now. While it may be age-appropriate for a preschooler to simply learn and recite that "Jesus died on the cross to save sinners," as our children age and mature we need to provide them a more in-depth biblical foundation for understanding the necessity of Jesus' death and what it accomplished.

After all, throughout history we can find thousands of heroic examples of men and women who willingly died for the sake of others. Some were Christians, but many were not. Only one life and death stands apart from all others—the perfect life and sacrificial death of God's holy and righteous Son.

11

Therefore, our children must be taught this essential doctrine. Salvation itself hangs on the truth and meaning of justification. And His glorious resurrection is the final seal of approval of this justifying work on behalf of God's people. May we diligently teach and remind our children the essentials of the Reformation, as expressed in the five "solas":

Salvation is by grace alone, through faith alone, in Christ alone, on the authority of Scripture alone, for the glory of God alone!

> **GATHER:** The topic of justification is so important that a few simple props are recommended to help explain the meaning of justification during the Instruct the Mind portion of this devotion. Be sure to prepare the props and practice with them ahead of time.
> You will need a clear plastic bag (e.g., 1 gallon-size storage bag), one piece of white paper, a table in the middle of the group, a permanent marker, one piece of dark-colored paper, a pair of scissors, a light-colored cloth or towel, and a trash can. You will also need a piece of paper and pencil or pen for the Pique Their Interest section.

PIQUE THEIR INTEREST

Depending on the size of your family and the age of your children, divide your family into teams (or simply work together as one team). Each team must have one proficient writer and will need a piece of paper and a pencil or pen. Explain that you are going to have a quick contest. Each team will have exactly one minute to do the following:

> Write as many words or phrases as you can think of that describe who Jesus is, and any words that describe something He has done.

Give the signal to begin and end. Take a minute to quickly read each team's answers.

INSTRUCT THE
MIND

Introduce, read, and interact with the following Scriptures:

The New Testament Scriptures introduce us to the Person, teachings, and deeds of Jesus. We learn about who Jesus is: From all eternity, He has existed as fully God. He is the second member of the Trinity along with God the Father and God the Holy Spirit. Yet, He also became fully human and was born of the virgin Mary. As truly God and truly man, Jesus lived a sinless life—perfectly obeying and fulfilling God's holy and righteous law.

We read of His many miracles—healing the sick, blind, and lame. Feeding thousands of hungry people with a few pieces of food. Even raising the dead to life again. All of these miracles were glorious deeds done to show that He was truly the LORD God.

We read about His teaching through parables, illustrations, a sermon, and commands, all of which point to the greatness and worth of God and our need to fear, honor, love, and obey Him. Jesus also made great claims about Himself—claims that showed why God the Father had sent Him into the world. Here is just one of these claims:

> *Jesus said…, "I am the way, and the truth, and the life. No one comes to the Father except through me."*—JOHN 14:6

What is the meaning of this claim? [Jesus is the only way to God. You can't be in a right relationship with God apart from Jesus.]

But how did Jesus accomplish this? How did Jesus become the one and only way for sinners to become right with a holy God? (Encourage a few responses.)

Listen very carefully as I read one of the most important paragraphs in the Bible.[1]

---

[1] If you have younger children and this passage is too difficult, the following verses could be used to convey the key themes as you use the props: 2 Corinthians 5:21; 1 Peter 2:24; 1 John 2:2; and Ephesians 2:8-9.

11

*But now the righteousness of God has been
manifested apart from the law, although the
Law and the Prophets bear witness to it—
*²²*the righteousness of God through faith in Jesus
Christ for all who believe. For there is no distinction:
*²³*for all have sinned and fall short of the glory
of God,* ²⁴*and are justified by his grace as a gift,
through the redemption that is in Christ Jesus,
*²⁵*whom God put forward as a propitiation by
his blood, to be received by faith. This was to
show God's righteousness, because in his divine
forbearance he had passed over former sins.
*²⁶*It was to show his righteousness at the present
time, so that he might be just and the justifier
of the one who has faith in Jesus.*
—ROMANS 3:21-26

To explain what these verses mean, we are going to use some ordinary objects.

Display the CLEAR PLASTIC BAG.

These verses refer to God's "righteousness" four times. God is righteous. Everything He does is right. Let's pretend for a moment that this clear bag represents God being completely righteous, without any sin.

(Place the WHITE PIECE OF PAPER on the TABLE and use the MARKER to write the word "Me" in the center of the paper.)

❓ **But what about you and me? What do these verses tell us about our condition?** [We fall short of the glory of God. We are sinners.]

We are all sinners who have failed to love and honor God as we should. We have failed to keep God's law and commands. Therefore, we cannot be "justified"—be made right with God through the law. Our hearts are darkened with sin, and we are completely helpless to change this condition.

(Use the SCISSORS to quickly cut out a large heart shape from the DARK-COLORED PAPER. Place this HEART on top of the word "Me" on the WHITE PAPER)

Let's pretend for a moment that this dark heart represents our sin.

11

❓ **What has God decided is the right punishment for sin?** [death and hell, experiencing God's fierce anger—His wrath]

But in our last devotion we learned that, in the Old Testament, God had made a way for His people to be forgiven, showing God's mercy—His kindness toward undeserving sinners.

❓ **What did God instruct them to do?** [kill animals] **Why?** [to show that the right punishment for sin is death; something must die for sinners to be forgiven] By instructing His people to do this, God was showing "forbearance"—or patience—as He "passed over former sins." In other words, God "covered" their sins for a time by using the blood of animals as a substitute.

Place the LIGHT-COLORED CLOTH on top of the DARK HEART.

But the blood of animals could never "take away" sin. Therefore, animal sacrifices were only temporary. God had planned from all eternity to provide the perfect, final solution—one that would take away the sin of His people once and for all.

Write "Jesus" in large letters on the CLEAR BAG with the MARKER.

God's solution was to send His Son Jesus into the world. Jesus is fully God and is righteous, too. He showed this to be true by living a sinless life. He perfectly obeyed and fulfilled God's law and commands. Therefore, His name belongs on this clear plastic bag representing God's righteousness.

> *for all have sinned and fall short of the glory of God, ²⁴ and are justified by his grace as a gift, through the redemption that is Christ Jesus,*
>
> ROMANS 3:23-24

But let's look at the problem again. This "sin"—though covered up—is still there.

Remove the LIGHT-COLORED CLOTH from the DARK HEART and set the cloth aside.

This is where this really important phrase comes in from Romans 3:24b-25a…

11

> *...Christ Jesus, [25] whom God put forward*
> *as a propitiation by his blood,*—ROMANS 3:24B-25A

❓ **What do you think this verse means?** (Encourage a few responses.)
Here is a clue...

Draw a large, simple cross on the CLEAR BAG with the MARKER, and then place the DARK HEART within the bag. Also, if your children are using the *Glorious God, Glorious Gospel Notebook*, have them draw a cross after the words "God's solution for man's sin problem."

> The word "propitiation" means to fully receive and absorb God's wrath at sin in such a way that the punishment for sin is completely satisfied, so God can now show His favor. That is what Jesus did for His sinful people when He bled and died on the cross. He took away their sin.

Remove the DARK HEART from the PLASTIC BAG. Give it to a child and instruct him to quickly throw it in the TRASH CAN.

> But Jesus doesn't just take away sins. He also gives His people something that they need. Jesus gives to them His perfect righteousness.

Place the EMPTY CLEAR PLASTIC BAG on top of the WHITE PAPER so that the word "Me" is visible.

> So now God looks at His people through Jesus' payment on the cross. He sees them as forgiven, righteous, and "Not guilty." Jesus' resurrection from the dead is proof that He accomplished this. Therefore, God's people will never have to fear God's wrath. God's people are justified and redeemed through what Jesus has done. It is completely apart from anything we have done. That is why we are reminded in the passage that it is "by his grace as a gift" (Romans 3:24).

❓ **How does a person receive this gift?** [by faith in Jesus, believing in Him]

> Here is how our Romans 3:21-26 passage states this...

> *...through faith in Jesus Christ for*
> *all who believe.* (verse 22)
> *... received by faith.* (verse 25)
> *... the one who has faith in Jesus.* (verse 26)

SUMMARY

Jesus came into the world to do what we could never do. Jesus came to save His sinful people from God's righteous judgment. Jesus took the sin of His people and died in our place. Jesus experienced the wrath of God so that His people could experience lasting joy in God. Jesus came to be the perfect Law-keeper in our place. Jesus came to proclaim to sinners the most wonderful news in the world: There is salvation in Jesus! That is the good news of the Gospel.

ENGAGE THE HEART

Choose one or more of the following topics to discuss:

JESUS, THE SINLESS GOD-MAN

What are some of the commands of God? Can you keep all of them all the time? Do you think that any person could? What does it tell you about Jesus that He could perfectly keep the law? Why did God have to send His own Son to pay for sin, remove the wrath of God, and declare those who trust in Jesus righteous? What does this tell you about the heart of man? What does this tell you about the heart of God? What does this tell you about the heart of Jesus?

Make sure your children understand that not only was Jesus loving, humble, and self-sacrificing, but He was also submissive to the Father and trusted the Father's plan. You may want to look at Philippians 2:5-8.

JESUS, THE ONLY WAY TO GOD

What are some ways people believe we can earn the favor of God? Why is this wrong thinking?

Make sure your children understand that not only is it unbiblical thinking, and therefore untrue, but it is also impossible that man could do enough good to satisfy God's standards of righteousness.

11

Some people think that it is arrogant to believe that there is only one way to God. **Why is this untrue?**

What heart attitudes does it require to accept that Jesus is the only way to God? [humility, trust, conviction, brokenness, surrender, dependency] **How do you obtain** (get) **these heart attitudes?**

Make sure that your child understands that the heart that leads to salvation is a changed heart that only comes as a gift of God's grace. Though a child cannot change his heart, he can pray for a changed heart and ask for the grace to resist the sins of pride, unbelief and self-sufficiency.

A TEMPORARY SUBSTITUTE AND A PERMANENT SOLUTION

How does God's covering of man's sin through the blood of animals demonstrate God's patience? Think of the sins you have committed this week, this month, this year, in your lifetime. **Why was the blood of animals insufficient for Israel and for you?**

Can you imagine what it was like for Jesus to absorb the wrath of God for the sinful man? What does this tell you about sin? About Jesus? Why is the satisfactory substitute of Jesus' righteousness and the favor of God such a gift? Explain. How much of an impact does the death of Jesus on the cross make on your own heart? Explain. How can you grow in appreciation for the cross?

PERFECT RIGHTEOUSNESS AND JUSTIFICATION

If you are trusting in Jesus as your Savior, do you see yourself as having perfect righteousness? Explain. Is it hard to believe that God could look at you as forgiven, righteous, and not guilty? Explain. What may rob Christians of their joy in forgiveness? What lies might a Christian believe about his condition? How can you fight this?

If you are not trusting in Jesus as your Savior, does the weight of your sin trouble you? How will you answer a holy God about your sin? Does this strike fear and dread in your heart? Why or why not? How can your family pray for you?

FAITH IN JESUS

11

What does "faith in Jesus" or "believing in Jesus" mean? What is involved in trusting Jesus for the forgiveness of sin?

Make sure your child understands that true faith in Jesus produces repentance for sin—not just sorrow over bad behavior but a recognition of the true nature of a sinful heart and its inability to change apart from grace. Faith involves not just the intellectual understanding but a deep-in-the-heart conviction that Jesus is the only One who can make things right with God and give him the righteousness that makes him acceptable to God. True faith produces the desire to follow Jesus in obedience and to "count everything as loss because of the surpassing worth of knowing Christ Jesus" (Philippians 3:8). It means surrendering your desires to Jesus and seeing Him as the greatest treasure. It involves a hunger to know Jesus better, to read His Word, and walk in obedience to His ways.

INFLUENCE THE WILL

What action or actions will you take this week to examine your heart and ask God to show you if you have saving faith? How can you grow in appreciation for the patience of God, the provision of God, and the sacrifice made by Jesus on the cross?

FAMILY WORSHIP TIME

Read the words of the hymn "Before the Throne of God Above" by Vikki Cook and Charitie Lees Bancroft (*Hymns of Grace*, 187, or find it on the internet). How do the words convey the sense of standing in a courtroom? What is the sinner's plea in this situation? Why? What confidence and assurance is communicated in this hymn? Sing the hymn together.

Jesus saves us for living a whole new kind of life—life "in Christ," united with Him. It involves daily recognizing Jesus' authority in our lives as we

TRUST HIS WAYS

are best, right, and good for us.

DAILY WALKING WITH JESUS

INTRODUCTION FOR PARENTS

Many people are longing for a Savior but few are longing for a Lord and Master. Jesus, as a Savior who saves us from the wrath of God and promises eternal life, is an appealing prospect for troubled souls. But that He should also be Lord and Master over our lives...well, that's not so appealing to many. Yet, Jesus is not divisible. He is the one and only Savior, and is also Lord and Master. All authority has been given to Him, and all who come to Him must gladly bow in submission to Him. In other words, there is a high "cost" to the gift of salvation that Jesus freely offers to those who repent and believe. We must bid our children to carefully consider the cost. Trusting in Jesus is not simply a decision to ask Him for forgiveness of sins; it's a call to follow Him for a lifetime.

Consider for a moment these words from Jesus:

> *The Jesus told his disciples, "If anyone would come after me, let him deny himself and take up his cross and follow me."*—MATTHEW 16:24

This active, daily, grace-dependent, Spirit-empowered submission to Jesus and His ways is the mark of a true disciple. It involves gladly surrendering our ways to His ways. It is living out the "new self" in union with Christ. It is sanctification—the ongoing work of God in His children, in which we strive to become more and more like Jesus, righteous and holy. Furthermore, it's important to emphasize and model for our children that submission to Jesus and His ways does not serve to squash our joy—it enables our joy. Jesus' ways, while at times difficult and filled with momentary suffering, lead us in paths of righteousness in which we experience the pleasure of our Father's smile in our daily lives and eagerly await the promise of eternal joy in the life to come.

12

> **GATHER:** Piece of paper with "FOLLOW" written on it in big letters; for each two people in your family—piece of paper, pen or pencil, and rubber band or string

PIQUE THEIR INTEREST

OPTION 1—Before beginning this devotion, write "FOLLOW" in large letters on a PIECE OF PAPER. (Your family should not see or know about this word before you begin.) Place this FOLLOW SIGN face down on the table. Explain that you are going to do a short experiment. Divide the family into pairs. If possible, pair a non-writer with a writer. Give each pair a PIECE OF PAPER. Next, give the designated writer of the pair a PEN OR PENCIL. Finally, use a RUBBER BAND or something similar to join the writer's hand (at the wrist) with the hand of the other person. (The rubber band does not need to be tight for the experiment to work.) Finally, instruct the non-writers to close their eyes. While they do so, reveal the word you have previously written on the FOLLOW SIGN to the writer of each pair. Place the FOLLOW SIGN face down on the table again. The non-writers can open their eyes again. Now instruct the writers to write the word on their PIECE OF PAPER as quickly as possible.

OPTION 2—Describe the preceding illustration, or demonstrate it with the help of the youngest child in the family as non-writer, and you as the writer.

? Which member of your team seemed to be the "leader" in this experiment? Why? Did the non-writer help or hinder in any way? Why was this important to the outcome?

We are going to quickly review what we learned about the Gospel in our last devotion, and then see how this writing illustration can help us understand something important about the Christian life.

INSTRUCT THE
MIND

Introduce, read, and interact with the following Scriptures:

In the previous devotion, we learned that the Gospel is the good news that God offers salvation for sinners through His Son, Jesus. Here is a very quick summary of what Jesus did: Jesus lived a perfectly righteous and holy life—a sinless life. Yet Jesus died on the cross in place of His sinful people, receiving God's wrath in our place, so that we could be forgiven. In doing so, He gives to His people His perfect righteousness in place of our sin. Then, Jesus rose from the dead, proving He had satisfied God's justice. Because of what Jesus has done, His people will receive eternal life—glorifying and enjoying God forever.

Salvation is by grace alone—God's free gift, and must be received through faith—trusting in who Jesus is and what He has done for you.

❓ But is that the end of the story? If a person comes to faith in Jesus, can you just simply say something like, "I have trusted in Jesus to save me. I am forgiven of my sin and will go to heaven someday," and then just go on with your day-to-day life as usual? (Encourage a few responses.)

> *I have been crucified with Christ. It is no longer I who live, but Christ who lives in me. And the life I now live in the flesh I live by faith in the Son of God, who loved me and gave himself for me.*—GALATIANS 2:20

❓ What does this verse mean? Does a Christian simply say, "I trust Jesus," and then go on living the same as before? (Encourage a few responses.)

Think for a moment of our beginning illustration. One person was "joined" to the other. The person doing the writing had the "lead." That person knew the word and knew what to do. The other person's job was to yield and follow that lead. This can help us understand what it means to truly have faith in Jesus. If you are a Christian, you are now in Christ, meaning you are "united" or "joined" to Him. Here are a few words from Jesus that summarize what this looks like. Listen carefully for action words—words that describe something to do.

> ..."If anyone would come after me,
> let him deny himself and take up his cross
> and follow me."—MATTHEW 16:24

> "Take my yoke upon you, and learn
> from me,"—MATTHEW 11:29A

> "If you love me, you will obey
> what I command."—JOHN 14:15 (NIV 1984)

> "By this my Father is glorified, that you bear much
> fruit and so prove to be my disciples."—JOHN 15:8

What action words did you hear in these verses? [deny, take up, follow, learn, love, obey, bear] **How would you summarize the kind of life Jesus is talking about?** [Some possible responses: We are to do things Jesus' way, and not our own way. The Christian life will be difficult at times. Obedience to Jesus is not optional; it shows true love for Him. Christians will "bear fruit"—they give outward proof of being Jesus' disciples.]

Why is it right and good that a Christian should learn from, submit to, obey, and follow Jesus? [Some possible responses: He is God and has total authority over our lives. He is the only one who has already lived a righteous and holy life. His ways are the only ways that can make us truly happy.]

I am going to quickly read some other verses about living as a Christian. As I read, listen carefully again for action words. See if you can keep track of how many you hear.

> ...put off your old self, which belongs to your
> former manner of life and is corrupt through
> deceitful desires,—EPHESIANS 4:22

> ...put on the new self, created after the
> likeness of God in true righteousness
> and holiness.—EPHESIANS 4:24

but as he who called you is holy, you also be
holy in all your conduct,—1 PETER 1:15

For we are God's workmanship, created in Christ
Jesus to do good works...—EPHESIANS 2:10A (NIV 1984)

Do not be conformed to this world, but be
transformed by the renewal of your mind, that by
testing you may discern what is the will of God, what
is good and acceptable and perfect.—ROMANS 12:2

for at one time you were darkness,
but now you are light in the Lord.
Walk as children of light.—EPHESIANS 5:8

Here is a summary of the key action words. See if you noted them:

<u>Put off</u> your old self.

<u>Put on</u> your new self.

<u>Be</u> holy in all your conduct.

<u>Do</u> good works.

<u>Do not</u> be conformed to this world.

<u>Be</u> transformed by the
renewal of your mind.

[<u>Test</u> and] <u>discern</u> what is the will of God.

<u>Walk</u> as children of light.

Would you say that being a follower of Jesus is easy or difficult? Explain your answer. (Encourage a few responses.)

Here is how the apostle Paul talked about being a follower of Jesus:

But now that you have been set free from sin
and have become slaves of God,
the fruit you get leads to sanctification
and its end, eternal life.—ROMANS 6:22

12

❓ **What is meant by having become "slaves of God"?** [If you are a Christian, God owns you. You should see Jesus as your Lord and Master. You are to live to please Him.]

Being a "slave of God" leads to something called "sanctification." Sanctification is the ongoing work of God in His children, in which they strive to become more and more like Jesus, slowly but surely. The more sanctified we become, the greater will be our joy, because living according to God's design gives the greatest satisfaction.

❓ **What is at the end of sanctification?** [eternal life]

SUMMARY

The Gospel is the good news that Jesus came into the world to save God's people from the judgment we deserve. This salvation is by God's grace alone, through faith in Jesus alone. But Jesus doesn't simply save His people *from* God's judgment, He also saves us *for* something. Jesus saves us for living a whole new kind of life—life "in Christ," united with Him. It involves daily recognizing Jesus'

> Sanctification is the ongoing work of God in His children, in which they strive to become more and more like Jesus, slowly but surely. The more sanctified we become, the greater will be our joy, because living according to God's design gives the greatest satisfaction.

authority in our lives. He is not just a Savior; He is also Lord and Master. It means loving and trusting that His ways are best, right, and good for us. It means learning from Him by reading His Word and seeing how He lived. It means submitting to and obeying His commands. At times, it will mean making really hard choices that may bring us temporary hurt and pain. Following Jesus in this way is a long slow process in which a Christian grows to become more and more like Jesus—to become more holy and righteous. Following Jesus in this way isn't just for today and tomorrow. It means following Him your entire life, even to old age, even until death. And, at death, Jesus promises that His disciples will receive the prize of eternal life, enjoying His fellowship forever and ever.

ENGAGE THE
HEART

Choose one or more of the following topics to discuss.

CRUCIFIED WITH CHRIST

Being crucified with Christ means that something has died. **What has died for those who are crucified with Christ?** [our former manner of life; the striving after the world and sin] **If you are a Christian, what changes do you see in yourself since you trusted Jesus as your Savior? What does the phrase "Christ lives in me" mean?**

Make sure your child understands that not only does the Holy Spirit live in the Christian, giving him the desire for righteousness, but also the power to resist sin. Also, Christians now become representatives of Christ—an example to the world of what Christ is like as we become more like Christ.

What does it mean to "live by faith in the Son of God"? Give a practical example of living by faith in a particular situation. (For example: Suppose you have lost your job. Living by faith in Christ means that you commit your financial problems and your need for a new job to Christ. You resist the sins of worry, anger, and envy and instead trust that God has a good and right plan for your life. You trust that God will "supply every need… according to his riches in glory in Christ Jesus," as it says in Philippians 4:19.)

SUBMISSION

What is submission? [bending your will to the will of another; giving up your desires to fulfill the desires of another] **Why is submission so hard for us? What does submission require?**

Make sure your child understands that submission not only requires the willingness to give up one's own will, but it also requires trust, confidence, and love for the one to whom we are submitting.

What is your biggest struggle in submitting to Christ? Explain. **How can we pray for you?**

PRAYER TIME

What struggles do you face in submitting to Christ?

12

PUT OFF, PUT ON

What does it mean to "put off your old self"? What kinds of thoughts, desires, words, and actions must a person who is in Christ put off? What are some of the things you personally must put off? What is one thing you can ask God to help you put off or fight to put off, and for which we can pray for you?

What does it mean to "put on the new self"? What does the new self look like? Be specific. What is one thing you desire to put on with the help of Christ? Practically, what steps can you take to fight the fight of faith and put on the new self in this area?

SANCTIFICATION

Sanctification is the process of becoming more like Christ. **What does the word "process" imply?** If you are a Christian, look back over the past few years. **Where can you see the work of God in sanctifying you?** Praise God together with your family for God's grace, and ask Him to complete His good work in you.

ETERNAL LIFE

God has promised His children a great reward—a fully sanctified (glorified) **eternal life with Him. What do you think this will be like?** (Imagine what it will be like to live in community with God and fully sanctified people. What will be present? What will not be present?)

The Bible says that Jesus was able to endure the cross by looking ahead to the joy (or the reward) **that was before him** (Hebrews 12:2). **How can looking forward to eternal life help you fight sin in your life and cooperate with the work of the Holy Spirit in sanctifying you? Practically, how can you look ahead to eternal life?**

INFLUENCE THE WILL

If you are a Christian, what action or actions will you take to work in cooperation with the Holy Spirit to submit to Christ, putting off the old and putting on the new in the process of sanctification? If you are not a Christian, what action can you take to discover the joy of the sanctified life, and to pray for the desire to be crucified with Christ?

FAMILY WORSHIP TIME

Read the words of the hymn, "We Come, O Christ, to You" by Margaret Clarkson (*Hymns of Grace*, 111, or find it on the internet). As you read the words, have your children raise their hands or speak out when they hear special words or phrases describing who Jesus is and/or His character. **What types of responses does the hymn call us to make because of who Jesus is and what He is like?** Sing the hymn together.

God's Word and the Holy Spirit work together in the life of a Christian, giving us the tools and help we need to **FOLLOW JESUS,** *every single day.*

114

EVERYTHING NEEDED FOR WALKING WITH JESUS

13

INTRODUCTION FOR PARENTS

The Christian life is similar to running a marathon. It requires training, discipline, and a long-term perspective and commitment. Putting indwelling sin to death, denying our own selfish desires, recognizing and protecting ourselves from Satan's fiery darts, and choosing to submit and follow Jesus' commands and ways are daily, ongoing struggles in this life. Sanctification is plain hard work that will continue throughout this present life and, apart from God's provision and power, a believer would be completely helpless. But God does not leave His children without the help we so desperately need.

First, God has given us His never-changing and always relevant Truth—the Bible. The Bible applies to every situation and circumstance in our lives. It is an undefeatable sword for fighting the fight of faith. Second, God has given every believer the gift of the Holy Spirit—the Holy Spirit dwelling *within* us. God *dwells* in us to give insight and understanding regarding the truths of Scripture. God dwells in us to convict, guide, comfort, and empower us. The Holy Spirit provides constant encouragement in our daily lives. He is the seal and guarantee of our new life in Christ. He gives wise counsel in any situation and, through Christ, He gives us constant access to our heavenly Father in the act of prayer. Truly God has given His children everything that is needed for a life of godliness!

PIQUE THEIR INTEREST

Pose the following scenario:

> Suppose I told you to do a really difficult job like _painting the house, or something else appropriate for your family's situation_ . **What would you hope that I would keep in mind?** [your age, your ability, the need for help and instruction, etc.]
>
> **What kind of tools would you need to do the job successfully?** [paint, brushes, rollers, etc.] **Do you think that I would provide you with those tools, or would I expect you to get them on your own? Why would I provide them for you?** [because you know that your child cannot provide these without your help]
>
> Loving parents want good for their children. We desire that you grow up and learn important skills and habits that will help you lead a productive and happy life. But we also know that you cannot do this on your own. You need help. Good parents provide the tools and the help their children need.

INSTRUCT THE
MIND

Introduce, read, and interact with the following Scripture:

> In the last devotion, we learned about something called "sanctification." Sanctification is the ongoing process in which a Christian—a child of God—grows to become more and more like Jesus. Christians become more like Jesus in their thoughts, desires, words, and actions. They become more holy and righteous. This involves daily denying their own selfish and sinful ways, and doing things Jesus' way instead. Sanctification is for a lifetime, and it is really hard work.

? **Do you think God offers any kind of tools or help for His children?** Explain your answer.

13

His divine power has granted [given]
to us all things that pertain [belong]
to life and godliness,—2 PETER 1:3A

How does this verse answer the previous question? [God has given His children everything they need in order to be godly and follow Jesus.]

What do you think is meant by the "all things" that a Christian has been given? What tools or help would be needed to daily follow Jesus? (Encourage some responses.)

13

[Jesus said,] *"If you love me, you will keep my commandments.* ¹⁶ *And I will ask the Father, and he will give you another Helper, to be with you forever,* ¹⁷ *even the Spirit of truth, whom the world cannot receive, because it neither sees him nor knows him. You know him, for he dwells with you and will be in you...* ²⁶ *...he will teach you all things and bring to your remembrance all that I have said to you."*—JOHN 14:15-17, 26B

What help has God given His children? [the Holy Spirit] What is special about the Holy Spirit? [He dwells in God's people forever. He is given so that Jesus' disciples can remember, understand, and obey His commands.]

The Holy Spirit is the third member of the Trinity, along with God the Father and God the Son. The Holy Spirit is truly and fully God. Therefore, He is all-powerful.

> **The Holy Spirit is given so that Jesus' disciples can remember, understand, and obey His commands.**

So, why is the power of the Holy Spirit living within God's children so amazing? [Every Christian has been given power to follow Jesus in every situation. They never can say, "I can't fight against sin," or "Satan made me do it." He gives Christians the strength to put sin to death and obey Jesus.]

Here is something Paul says about living by the power of the Holy Spirit:

> *But I say, walk by the Spirit, and you will not gratify*
> *the desires of the flesh [your sinful nature]...*
> *²²...the fruit of the Spirit is love, joy, peace,*
> *patience, kindness, goodness, faithfulness,*
> *²³gentleness, self-control; against such things*
> *there is no law.—GALATIANS 5:16, 22-23*

13

If you are listening to the Holy Spirit and acting with His power, this will be shown by a certain kind of evidence—"fruit"—in your life. This fruit is holy and righteous and pleasing to God.

But, along with the help of the Holy Spirit, God has also given His children a powerful "tool" in the work of sanctification. The Holy Spirit "works" together with something in order to produce godly fruit in our lives.

> *All Scripture is breathed out by God and*
> *profitable for teaching, for reproof, for correction,*
> *and for training in righteousness, ¹⁷that the*
> *man of God may be complete, equipped for*
> *every good work.—2 TIMOTHY 3:16-17*

❓ **What equips a Christian for every good work?** [Scripture, the Bible] **In what four ways does it equip us?** [by teaching us, reproving us by telling us what is wrong and sinful, offering correction for doing what is right, and training us for righteous living]

So, God's Word and the Holy Spirit work together in the life of a Christian, giving us the tools and help we need to follow Jesus, every single day. We need the Holy Spirit and God's Word to grow. And we also need the protection they provide.

❓ **Do you remember Paul describing a certain type of armor—the type of armor and equipment a soldier would have? What was he talking about?** [putting on the armor of God for protection from Satan and his schemes]

> *Finally, be strong in the Lord and in the strength of*
> *his might. ¹¹Put on the whole armor of God, that you*
> *may be able to stand against the schemes of the devil.*

12 For we do not wrestle against flesh and blood, but against the rulers, against the authorities, against the cosmic powers over this present darkness, against the spiritual forces of evil in the heavenly places. 13 Therefore take up the whole armor of God, that you may be able to withstand in the evil day, and having done all, to stand firm. 14 Stand therefore, having fastened on the belt of truth, and having put on the breastplate of righteousness, 15 and, as shoes for your feet, having put on the readiness given by the gospel of peace. 16 In all circumstances take up the shield of faith, with which you can extinguish all the flaming darts of the evil one; 17 and take the helmet of salvation, and the sword of the Spirit, which is the word of God, 18 praying at all times in the Spirit, with all prayer and supplication…—EPHESIANS 6:10-18A

13

SUMMARY

God is a perfect, loving, good, and wise heavenly Father. God does not expect something from His children that He does not provide for them. He has provided everything needed to daily grow in becoming more and more like Jesus. God has given His children two amazing gifts—the Holy Spirit and His Word, which work together to guide, empower,

> God has given His children two amazing gifts—the Holy Spirit and His Word, which work together to guide, empower, and help us in the hard work of sanctification.

and help us in the hard work of sanctification. The Holy Spirit and God's Word also protect us from any schemes of Satan. Satan can never harm God's children. But God also expects His children to learn to make "use" of the Holy Spirit and His Word by putting these "tools" into action. For example, a Christian must take time to read God's Word and ask the Holy Spirit for help in understanding and applying it. When you are in a difficult situation, you should stop and ask the Holy Spirit to guide you, and ask for His power to do what is right and pleasing to Jesus. The more a Christian does this, the more we are trained for godly living. And godly living not only brings great pleasure to God, but also brings greater joy to us as we follow Jesus.

ENGAGE THE
HEART

Choose one or more of the following topics to discuss:

DIVINE POWER

13

His divine power has granted [given]
to us all things that pertain [belong] *to*
life and godliness,—2 PETER 1:3A

2 Peter 1:3a sounds like an overstatement if you forget the significance of the words "His divine power." **How do these words make this statement a reality? If God's unlimited power has given us all that we need to live a godly life, then why do we sin?**

Make sure your child understands that God's divine power is available to the believer, but we often neglect to depend on God and try to live the Christian life on our own power. Though we will never fully depend on God at all times, we can learn little by little to depend on Him more.

What holds you back from relying on God? How can you learn to depend on God's power rather than relying on yourself?

THE HOLY SPIRIT

John 14 tells us that for Christians, the Holy Spirit is our Helper. He will be with us forever, always testifies to the truth, and will teach us what we need and help us to remember the truth. **How often do you hear of the work of the Holy Spirit in your church?** Sometimes, we tend to neglect the help the Holy Spirit has to offer us. **If you are a Christian, how can you be more aware of depending on the Holy Spirit and leaning on Him as your helper?**

FRUITS OF THE SPIRIT

But I say, walk by the Spirit, and you will not gratify
the desires of the flesh [your sinful nature]
²²...the fruit of the Spirit is love, joy, peace,
patience, kindness, goodness, faithfulness,
²³gentleness, self-control; against such things
there is no law.—GALATIANS 5:16, 22-23

Describe practically, in real-life situations, the different fruits of the Spirit. (What does love look like in real life? What does patience look like in your relationships within your family? What does self-control look like in your habits? Etc.) **What fruit of the Holy Spirit do you see developing in your life?** Explain. **What fruit would you like to see formed in you? What are some practical steps you can take to grow in the fruit of the Spirit?**

13

SCRIPTURE

2 Timothy 3 tells us that all Scripture is profitable for us. However, if we do not know the Bible or if we do not apply it practically in our lives, we are not transformed by it. **Where are you lacking** (in knowledge, application, or both)? **Practically, how can you grow in your knowledge of the Bible? What does it mean to apply the Bible to your own life?** Give an example. **How can you grow in your application of the Word of God to your own life?**

THE ARMOR OF GOD

If we must put on God's armor, what does this imply? [We are in a spiritual battle.] **What does the word "schemes" mean? Are you often conscious that Satan is actually plotting, planning, and conniving to tempt you to sin? How can being aware of this help you? Do you think of life as a spiritual battle?** Think through your day and identify the spiritual battles that you faced. **Were you aware at the time that you were in a battle? What armor did you use? How can you be more aware of the spiritual battle you are in and be more conscious of putting on God's armor?**

PUTTING ON GOD'S ARMOR

What spiritual battles can this armor help your family fight?

Belt of Truth:

Breastplate of Righteousness:

Shoes of the Gospel of Peace:

13

Shield of Faith:

Helmet of Salvation:

Sword of the Spirit:

INFLUENCE THE WILL

What action or actions will you take to be more dependent on the Holy Spirit and to use the tools God has given you to fight the fight of faith?

FAMILY WORSHIP TIME

Read the words of the hymn, "A Mighty Fortress Is Our God" by Martin Luther (*Hymns of Grace*, 53, or find it on the internet). For older children, you may want to emphasize the importance of the Protestant Reformation 500 years ago and Martin Luther's role in it. As you read the words of the hymn, define any unfamiliar words. **What dangers are expressed in the hymn? Does Luther give any confidence in our own power or efforts to prevail in the Christian life? Why not? What does he point to as our one and only hope? How does he point to the importance of both the Holy Spirit and the Word of God? What "gifts" is he referring to in verse 4?** Sing the hymn together.

GROWING FRUIT DAY BY DAY

How is your family practically seeing the fruit of the Spirit in everyday life?

LOVE	JOY	PEACE
PATIENCE	**KINDNESS**	**GOODNESS**
FAITHFULNESS	**GENTLENESS**	**SELF-CONTROL**

The gathered church is to focus on three main goals: **WORSHIP** *of God,* **EQUIPPING** *and* **ENCOURAGING** *the saints for a life of godliness,* *and* **PROCLAIMING** *the Gospel to the lost.*

LIVING TOGETHER AS GOD'S FAMILY

INTRODUCTION FOR PARENTS

Jesus did not come to save His people so that they could live in personal, isolated "kingdoms." Jesus came to establish and build His church. Every child of God belongs to this *invisible* church. The Bible describes the church with various metaphors: a body, a dwelling place, a household, and a bride. These metaphors are meant to describe the position and way of life for every believer. We have not been saved into some type of impersonal establishment. There is a family intimacy that is to permeate God's people. Together as His people there are special privileges and responsibilities to be enjoyed and pursued in fellowship with one another. And God, in His gracious provision, has designed that this be experienced in visible, local churches. The gathered church is to focus on three main goals: worship of God, equipping and encouraging the saints for a life of godliness, and proclaiming the Gospel to the lost.

In a world that is increasingly hostile to Christ and those who follow Him, the church is an amazing gift. We can derive strength, comfort, and encouragement from one another. Furthermore, the family provides us with added help for our personal sanctification by provided teaching, counsel, correction, and motivation. Even if your children are not yet believers, it is important to give them a picture of family life among Christians. The more we, as believers, faithfully live out Christ's design for His church, the more attractive and appealing the family of God will be to them.

PIQUE THEIR INTEREST

Explain that you are going to have a quick contest. The family will have 30 seconds to call out as many answers as possible to the question:

What are some benefits of being a part of our family?

When the 30 seconds are up, ask:

If I had also asked you, "Are there any responsibilities that go along with being a part of our family?" would you have also been able to come up with some? Name a few.

14

Being a member of a family involves both special privileges and responsibilities. Both are really important. Both are meant to help us grow and mature. Both are meant to help us live a happy and fulfilling life.

INSTRUCT THE MIND

Introduce, read, and interact with the following Scripture:

The last two devotions have reminded us about the importance of following Jesus, day by day, throughout our entire lives. If you are a Christian, God expects you to grow up and mature, becoming more and more like Jesus. And, just like any good father provides help for his children to grow and mature, God provides everything needed for His children to grow in godliness.

❓ **What two special "tools" or help does God provide for His children that we learned about in the last devotion?** [the Holy Spirit and God's Word, the Bible]

But there is another means of help God has given His children. I am going to read a series of verses. They all have something in common. Listen carefully and, when I am finished reading, I will ask you to identify it.

*Love one another with brotherly
affection.*—ROMANS 12:10A

Bear one another's burdens,—GALATIANS 6:2A

*Outdo one another in
showing honor.*—ROMANS 12:10B

*...consider how to stir up one another
to love and good works,*—HEBREWS 10:24B

...serve one another.—GALATIANS 5:13B

Live in harmony with one another.—ROMANS 12:16A

*...confess your sins to one another
and pray for one another,*—JAMES 5:16A

*Be kind to one another, tenderhearted,
forgiving one another,*—EPHESIANS 4:32A

Show hospitality to one another...—1 PETER 4:9A

...instruct one another.—ROMANS 15:14B

...welcome one another...—ROMANS 15:7A

*...encourage one another and build
one another up,*—1 THESSALONIANS 5:11A

...comfort one another...—2 CORINTHIANS 13:11B

14

❓ **What repeated phrase, words, did all these verses have in common?** [one another] **Who is "one another"? Do you think it refers to just anyone you know or meet?** Explain your answer.

*For through him we both have access in one
Spirit to the Father. ¹⁹ So then you are no longer
strangers and aliens, but you are fellow citizens with
the saints and members of the household of God,
²⁰ built on the foundation of the apostles and
prophets, Christ Jesus himself being the cornerstone,
²¹ in whom the whole structure, being joined together,
grows into a holy temple in the Lord. ²² In him
you also are being built together into a dwelling
place for God by the Spirit.*—EPHESIANS 2:18-22

These verses define who is meant by all of the "one another" references.

❓ **Who is "one another"?** [members of the household of God, every Christian]

These verses are describing the church. The church is the household of God. Jesus is at work building the church. It is a "dwelling place" for God....not because it is an actual building made of bricks or wood or steel. The church is made up of people—every person who is trusting in Jesus for salvation. The church is the family of God and, because it is the most special family of all, God has given the church special privileges and responsibilities for living life together as God's children. Some of these privileges and responsibilities are mentioned in the "one another" verses that we read. All of these "one another" verses are commands for Christians to help other Christians grow to be more and more like Jesus.

14

Let's quickly look at just one of these commands.

> *...consider how to stir up one another*
> *to love and good works,*—HEBREWS 10:24B

❓ **What does it mean to "stir up" one another?** [to encourage someone, motivate someone, prod someone to do something] **What are Christians to stir up other Christians to do?** [to be loving and to do good works] **Why is this important?** (Encourage a few responses. You may want to remind them that Jesus saved us so that we might do good works for His glory.) **Why do we sometimes need to be "stirred up" in order to do this?** [We can grow lazy, unconcerned, uncaring, self-centered, or hardened. Other people can serve to encourage us and motivate us.]

SUMMARY

Jesus did not save sinners so that we could simply live on our own—trying to live the Christian life by ourselves. Jesus died and rose again in order to create a special family, God's family—the church. While the church does include every single Christian from all over the world, God has also given us local churches—smaller groups of Christians that come together on a regular basis and live out family life together. This is very important because, just as the Holy Spirit and God's Word help Christians grow in becoming more like Jesus, the members of Jesus' church are called to help one another, too. This is both a wonderful privilege and a special responsibility. If you are trusting in Jesus for your salvation, you are a member of His church—an important member of the family—and these privileges and responsibilities are for you, too. No matter how young or old, you are to live out "one another"

> **Jesus died and rose again in order to create a special family, God's family— the church.**

14

commands. For children, it may mean that you will be more on the "receiving end" of many of these, just like in our own family. This is meant to help you grow in your knowledge of God and your faith in Christ. And, as you grow, you should look for more and more ways you can live out the "one another" commands. Not only is this good for you, but it will help other Christians, too. Most of all, it is pleasing to the head of the family—God Himself.

ENGAGE THE HEART

Choose one or more of the following topics to discuss.

THE FAMILY OF GOD

In your own words, describe what a family should be. **What makes the family unique among human relations? How is the care for one another within the family unique?** (For example, how is the care of your parents different from how they care for your friends?) **Why is family so important?**

PRIVILEGES AND RESPONSIBILITIES

What privileges do you have because you are a member of our family? What responsibilities do you have within and for your family? **What is the result of enjoying the privileges without taking the responsibility?** (What would the relationships be like in our family if everyone tried to take advantage of the benefits but not fulfill their responsibilities?) **What privileges do you have if you are a child of God?**

"ONE ANOTHER" COMMANDS

14

God has given us responsibilities for each other within His family. Many of these responsibilities are noted in the New Testament letters. Look at the verses we read earlier. Choose some and state very practically what that can look like within our local church. Also, discuss the benefits believers receive when these commands are lived out. Then think of an individual or a family we can reach out to within the community of believers. Also, look at some of the specific questions associated with some of the commands.

Love one another with brotherly affection.—ROMANS 12:10A

Is there anyone you are failing to love in your church? What must you do about this?

Bear one another's burdens,—GALATIANS 6:2A

What are some of the particular burdens of people in our church? Is there something you can do to share one of these burdens? Can you give an example of another Christian helping you during a difficult time?

Outdo one another in showing honor.—ROMANS 12:10B

Is there anyone in your church you disrespect, make fun of, or shun (avoid or ignore)? **Why? Do you need to repent of your heart attitude? Do you need to ask forgiveness from anyone? How could you show honor to this person this week?**

...consider how to stir up one another to love and good works,—HEBREWS 10:24B

Do you encourage others to do what is right and follow God's ways? Has anyone encouraged you to love another or to act kindly toward someone else? How did they do this? (What was positive and helpful about the way this person encouraged you?) **Tell us about it. How can you follow this person's example?**

...serve one another.—GALATIANS 5:13B

Do you look for ways to serve in the church? What are you doing to serve others? How have you been served?

Live in harmony with one another.—ROMANS 12:16A

Is there anyone you have a broken relationship with? Have you done all that you can do to live in harmony with that person or to reconcile with him? Are there steps toward reconciliation you need to make?

...confess your sins to one another and pray for one another,
—JAMES 5:16A

Is there anything you need to confess? How do you need others to pray for you? Do you make it a habit to pray for others, too?

14

Be kind to one another, tenderhearted, forgiving one another,
—EPHESIANS 4:32A

Is there anyone you are holding a grudge against; anyone you need to forgive? What steps can you take? How have you experienced forgiveness when you have wronged someone? How did that make you feel?

Show hospitality to one another...—1 PETER 4:9A

Who can you show hospitality to? What might be one thing we could do as a family to show hospitality to someone at church that we don't know very well?

...instruct one another.—ROMANS 15:14B

Are you faithful in sharing God's Word with others? What responsibility do you take to instruct those who are younger or newer in faith than you are? Can you name some Christians who have taken time to teach you God's Word? How has their instruction helped you?

...welcome one another...—ROMANS 15:7A

Is there anyone new in your church who needs to be folded into the family? What can you do to help that person get connected and feel comfortable in the church?

...encourage one another and build one another up,
—1 THESSALONIANS 5:11A

Do you build up others or tear them down (e.g., gossip, ridicule—make fun of, criticize)? **How can you encourage them?**

Can you recall (remember and tell us about) **a time when someone was really helpful in strengthening your faith?**

...comfort one another...—2 CORINTHIANS 13:11B

Is there anyone in your church who needs comfort? What can your family do to ease this person's suffering? When something sad or difficult has happened in your own life, have you received comfort from other Christians? What did they do that was helpful?

14

INFLUENCE THE
WILL

What action or actions will you take to obey the "one another" commands?

FAMILY WORSHIP TIME

Read the words of the hymn, "Oh, How Good It Is" by Keith and Kristyn Getty, Ross Holmes, and Stuart Townend (*Hymns of Grace*, 332, or find it on the internet). Discuss the key themes of family life in each stanza. **What is the main focus of the chorus—what is the main goal of family life? Why is this important?** Sing the hymn together.

SERVE ONE ANOTHER

Brainstorm practical ways your family can serve people in these areas:

FAMILY

CHURCH

FRIENDS

NEIGHBORS

God has promised that one day, all of His children will be transformed, changed, and be given glorious bodies like Jesus' own body, so that we can joyfully love, honor, and praise God forever—never running out of ways to be

IN AWE OF HIM!

LIVING FOR THE GLORY OF GOD

INTRODUCTION FOR PARENTS

As we stated in the general introduction to this devotional study, we have been aiming to give an overview of the main message of the Bible—the Gospel. Although this study has not been exhaustive in its scope or depth, we have identified and explored the essential truths necessary for understanding the core of the Gospel. And we have addressed important questions, including: *Who is God and what is He like? Why do we exist? What is our greatest need and problem? How can we be saved? How should we now live?*

In this last devotion, we would like to end in a manner that ties everything together. The grand finale, so to speak, will be...The Goal of the Gospel. This is the goal for which everything exists and the ultimate meaning for all of life. Ponder these words for a moment:

> ...the highest, best, final, decisive good of the gospel, without which no other gifts would be good, is the glory of God in the face of Christ revealed for our everlasting enjoyment. The saving love of God is God's commitment to do everything necessary to enthrall us with what is most deeply and durably satisfying, namely himself.[1]

From the beginning of the Bible to the end, everything points us Godward. The Gospel exists to make us a holy people *for* God.

[1] Piper, John. *God Is the Gospel.* (Wheaton, Ill.: Crossway Books, 2005), 13.

Christ died to reconcile us *to God*. Christ rose from the dead to give us eternal life *with God*. We are sanctified by the Spirit and the Word in order to transform us into the image of the Son so that we might *glorify God* in everything we think, feel, say, and do. Everything is *from God and through God and to God*. To God be the glory forever!

PIQUE THEIR INTEREST

Pose the following scenario:

> Suppose you have experienced something really spectacular and exciting— *a sporting event, vacation destination, or other activity your children love* . It was the "best ever"—something to remember for a lifetime.

> **Would you want to tell your friends about it? Why? What kinds of words might you use in order to describe how great it was? Would your tone and body language also show your excitement? How so? What might be the effect on your friends? Would they be more likely to want to experience it themselves? Why?**

> We naturally tend to want to share exciting news with our friends and family. Our words, expressions, and tone all communicate how much we "love" or are "wowed" by something. We just can't keep it to ourselves. We are bursting to share it!

15

INSTRUCT THE
MIND

Read, and interact with the following Scripture:

> In our last devotion, we learned about the church—the family of God. We also learned about life in the family of God—how we are to help one another grow in the Christian life. But there is something important about life in the family of God that we didn't mention.

> Listen carefully to what the apostle Peter had to say about the church:

But you are a chosen race, a royal priesthood, a holy nation, a people for his own possession, that you may proclaim the excellencies of him who called you out of darkness into his marvelous light.—1 PETER 2:9

❓ **Peter describes the church in four different ways. What are they?** [a chosen race, a royal priesthood, a holy nation, a people for His own possession] **What are God's chosen people to do?**

They are to *"...proclaim the excellencies of him who called you out of darkness into his marvelous light."*

❓ **What does this mean?** (Encourage a few responses. For younger children, define "proclaim" as "to tell," and "excellencies of him" as "great things about God.")

Let's see how many excellencies—words describing God's greatness—we can call out in 20 seconds. [The list may include: holy, eternal, righteous, Creator, all-powerful, patient, loving, kind, good, merciful, worthy, wise, just, sovereign, etc.]

15

In a sense, every Christian, and the church as a whole, is to be "bursting" with words, descriptions, expressions, emotions, and actions that show everyone around us the greatness and worth of God. But Peter also adds a reminder: *"proclaim the excellencies of him who called you out of darkness into his marvelous light."*

❓ **What is this referring to?** [God saving and redeeming His people through the death of Jesus on the cross; God's people were once under His judgment and wrath, but now they are saved and will receive eternal life.]

God does not want the message of salvation in Jesus to be kept secret. The church—every Christian—has the greatest, best, and most exciting news of all to share.

> **God does not want the message of salvation in Jesus to be kept secret. The church—every Christian—has the greatest, best, and most exciting news of all to share.**

Think for a moment back to our beginning illustration of the ___exciting event___. You probably didn't have to be forced to get excited about it. That is because we all look for and crave things and experiences that bring us some kind of joy and delight. We want (and even need) to be "wowed" by something in order to be happy. God made us that way when He made us in His image and likeness. He made us to be wowed beyond measure, beyond what we can even imagine. But He also knows that there is only one thing in the entire universe that can wow us for a lifetime and bring true lasting joy and satisfaction: God Himself!

> **When we live with the knowledge and mindset that God is greatest and best...**
>
> **And when we give honor Him as the Most High God...**
>
> **And when we love Him as our most valuable treasure...**
>
> **And when we speak and act in ways that show this to be true...**
>
> **Then we are living in a way that glorifies Him and brings us lasting joy.**

15

That is the great purpose God created us for and the great purpose that Jesus saved us for—to bring glory to God in everything we think, feel, say, and do.

This is why the Bible says,

> *So, whether you eat or drink, or whatever you do, do all to the glory of God.*—1 CORINTHIANS 10:31

That is an amazing truth! Think about it for a minute:

If you eat an apple, you should do it in a way that glorifies God. It might mean thinking and saying something like, "God made this apple and it tastes absolutely delicious. Thank you, God. You are good!" or "God you are amazing—You put seeds inside apples so we would have more apples. You always provide for your people. You truly are a good and gracious God!"

If you are riding your bike, you should do it to the glory of God. "Thank you, Jesus, for the gift of this bike, and thank you for this beautiful day. You are the best!" Or "It is amazing how you made our legs to work so that I can pedal this bike. Thank you for giving me strong legs…and for all the wonderful ways you made the human body to work."

❓ **But do we always do all things for the glory of God? Why do you think that even Christians don't always glorify God as they should? Why do they sometimes express more honor, love, and praise for a sports star or game or new gadget or friend more than for God?** (Encourage a few responses.)

Even those who have been Christians for a long time do not glorify God perfectly as they should. That is because there is a final "finishing" step to the Christian life. Something that is yet to be seen and experienced.

But our citizenship is in heaven, and from it
we await a Savior, the Lord Jesus Christ,
²¹who will transform our lowly body to be like his
glorious body, by the power that enables him even to
subject all things to himself.—PHILIPPIANS 3:20-21

15

Beloved, we are God's children now, and what
we will be has not yet appeared; but we know
that when he appears we shall be like him,
because we shall see him as he is.—1 JOHN 3:2

❓ **If you are a Christian, where is your true and final home?** [heaven] **If you are a Christian, what will Jesus do to your body when you die?** [transform it to be like His glorious body] **What is meant by His "glorious" body?** [It will be a perfect body without sin. It will be like Jesus' resurrected body and last forever.] **Who will we finally be like in heaven?** [Jesus]

SUMMARY

God's people have been created, chosen, and saved for a very special purpose. Namely, we have been created in the image and likeness of God so that we might proclaim His excellencies in all of our thoughts, feelings, words, and actions. We are to be "wowed" and amazed by God more than anything or anyone else. Everything we do in life should demonstrate this. Everything should give glory to God. This is what will truly make us happy and give us joy forever.

God's people should be "bursting" with this news—wanting others to come to salvation in Jesus, too.

And yet we know that right now even Christians don't always glorify God the way they should. We are still experiencing the effects of sin. But God has promised that one day, all of His children will be transformed, changed, and be given glorious bodies like Jesus' own body, so that we can joyfully love, honor, and praise God forever—never running out of ways to be "wowed" by Him!

> We are to be "wowed" and amazed by God more than anything or anyone else. Everything we do in life should demonstrate this. Everything should give glory to God. This is what will truly make us happy and give us joy forever.

15

ENGAGE THE HEART

Choose one or more of the following topics to discuss.

A CHRISTIAN'S IDENTITY

What does it mean that, if you are a Christian, you are a "chosen race, a royal priesthood, a holy nation, a people for his own possession"? Try to think specifically of the implications of this description or identity that a Christian has.

Make sure your child understands the implications of being chosen—what it means to be a priesthood and to be royalty, what it means to be holy in your orientation, what it means to belong to God—to have Him as your Father.

In what ways can knowing this description of you, if you are a Christian, help you as you face some rejection or hurt in this world?

PROCLAIMING THE GOSPEL

Have you been "called out of darkness into his marvelous light"? Are you trusting in Jesus for salvation; have you received Him as your Lord and Master? If not, what holds you back? Why can't you depend on the fact that you may be growing up in a Christian home, or that you go to church? How can we pray for you?

Do you share the Gospel with others—the good news of salvation from sin and the wrath of God and the joy of being a child of God? If so, give an example. **If not, what holds you back?**

Practice sharing the Gospel message with each other.

3 PEOPLE OUR FAMILY WANTS TO SHARE THE GOSPEL WITH
and how we will overcome what is holding us back:

1. _____

2. _____

3. _____

15

DOING ALL TO THE GLORY OF GOD

1 Corinthians 10:31 tells us to do all to the glory of God. Think of some examples from ordinary life. **How can you take each opportunity to do all things "to the glory of God"?**

Make sure your child can come up with very specific examples from everyday life. Instruct him that doing something to the glory of God not only includes specifically what we do, but the heart attitude in which we do it. For example, two people can play a piano recital piece but with different heart attitudes—one with pride looking for the praise of man, and another with gratitude for God's musical gift, His grace and power to perform, and as an expression of praise to Him for "every good and perfect gift" that "comes from above." (See James 1:17.)

CITIZENSHIP

What is the meaning of "citizenship"? What are the privileges and responsibilities that come with citizenship? What is the difference between having a citizenship on earth and one in heaven? Give specific examples. How should remembering your heavenly citizenship (if you are a Christian) help you in the difficulties of this life?

Do some imagining...What will a transformed body be like? What will it be like to live in a world where there is no sin? What will it be like to see Jesus? What kinds of things would you like to say to Him when you see Him? What will you thank Him for? Spend some time praising God for the glorious gift of salvation and eternal life with Him.

15

INFLUENCE THE
WILL

What action or actions will you take to either 1) seek God with all your heart in the hope that He would make you His child, or 2) to live out your identity as a child of God and proclaim the Gospel to others?

FAMILY WORSHIP TIME

Find the words of the hymn, "Come Praise and Glorify" by Tim Chester and Bob Kauflin (*Hymns of Grace*, 44, or find it on the internet). Before reading the hymn, read Ephesians 1:3-14 on which the hymn is based. The text gives a type of succinct summary of the grand message of the Bible, the Gospel. As you read the hymn, what essential truths of the Gospel does it communicate? How do the beginning words of each verse and the chorus highlight the ultimate purpose of the Gospel? Why is this important to know? Sing the hymn together.

FOR GOD'S GLORY

Everyday situation: *How our family can do it for the glory of God:*

*...that the next
generations might*
**SET THEIR
HOPE IN GOD!**

TRUTH78

OUR VISION, MISSION, AND VALUES

Truth78 is a vision-oriented ministry for the next generations. We use the term "vision-oriented" to describe our ministry because we are aiming our children and youth toward an end goal and target. Our vision has been shaped by Psalm 78:1-7:

> Give ear, O my people, to my teaching;
> incline your ears to the words of my mouth!
> [2] I will open my mouth in a parable;
> I will utter dark sayings from of old,
> [3] things that we have heard and known,
> that our fathers have told us.
> [4] We will not hide them from their children, but tell to
> the coming generation the glorious deeds of the LORD,
> and his might, and the wonders that he has done.
> [5] He established a testimony in Jacob and
> appointed a law in Israel, which he commanded
> our fathers to teach to their children,
> [6] that the next generation might know them, the children
> yet unborn, and arise and tell them to their children,
> [7] so that they should set their hope in God and not
> forget the works of God, but keep his commandments.

These verses serve as a foundation for our vision for the next generations. They also guide our ministry's specific mission and the values that undergird and define our resources and training materials.

> **Our vision is that the next generations know, honor, and treasure God, setting their hope in Christ alone, so that they will live as faithful disciples for the glory of God.**

Our vision is that next generations will, by God's sovereign grace,

- come to genuinely **know** the truth of the triune God— Father, Son, and Holy Spirit—by becoming acquainted with His divine character, glorious deeds, redemptive work, and steadfast promises as revealed in His inerrant Word, the Bible.

- **honor** and revere God in a way befitting His incomparable greatness and worth.

- **treasure** God with undivided love and devotion, experiencing Him as their all-satisfying joy.

- set their full confidence and **hope in Christ alone**, who through His perfect life, sacrificial death, and victorious resurrection, reconciles sinners to God so that they might live as His covenant people.

- **live as faithful disciples** of Jesus through grace-dependent, Spirit-empowered obedience to His holy and righteous ways, which day by day progressively conforms them into His image and likeness so that they will bear fruit and stand mature in Christ.

- do everything **for the glory of God** by proclaiming His excellencies in all they think, say, and do so that His great name might receive all honor, thanksgiving, and praise!

> **Our mission is to nurture the faith of the next generations by equipping the church and home with resources and training that instruct the mind, engage the heart, and influence the will through proclaiming the whole counsel of God.**

To that end, we have developed resources and training that are undergirded and defined by the following values:

> God-centered, Bible-saturated,
> Gospel-focused, Christ-exalting,
> Spirit-dependent, doctrinally grounded,
> and discipleship-oriented.

RESOURCES
FOR CHURCH AND HOME

Truth78 offers the following resources and training materials for equipping the church and home:

VISION CASTING AND TRAINING

We offer a wide variety of booklets, video and audio seminars, articles, and other practical training resources that highlight and further expound our vision, mission, and values, as well as our educational philosophy and methodology. Many of these resources are freely distributed through our website. These resources and training serve to assist ministry leaders, volunteers, and parents in implementing Truth78's vision and mission in their churches and homes.

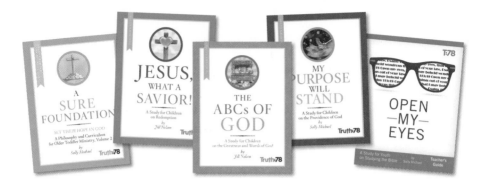

CURRICULUM

We publish materials designed for formal Bible instruction. The scope and sequence of these materials reflects our commitment to teach children and youth the whole counsel of God over the course of their education. Materials include curricula for Sunday school, Midweek Bible programs, Backyard Bible Clubs or Vacation Bible School, and Intergenerational studies. Most of these materials can be adapted for use in Christian schools and education in the home.

PARENTING AND FAMILY DISCIPLESHIP

We have produced a variety of materials and training resources designed to help parents in their role in discipling their children. These include booklets, video presentations, family devotionals, children's books (including the the Making HIM Known series published by P & R Publishing), articles, and other recommended resources. Furthermore, our curricula include Growing in Faith Together (GIFT) Pages to help parents apply what is taught in the classroom to their child's daily experience in order to nurture faith.

BIBLE MEMORY

Our Fighter Verses Bible memory program is designed to encourage churches, families, and individuals in the lifelong practice and love of Bible memory. The Fighter Verses program utilizes an easy-to-use Bible memory system with carefully chosen verses to help fight the fight of faith. It is available in print, on FighterVerses.com, and as an app for smart phones and other mobile devices. The Fighter Verses app includes review reminders, quizzes, songs, a devotional, and other memory helps. For pre-readers, Foundation Verses uses simple images to help young children memorize 76 key verses. We also offer a study, devotional guide, and coloring book that corresponds to the Set 1 of Fighter Verses. Visit FighterVerses.com for the weekly devotional blog and for free memory aids.

For more information on any of these resources and training materials contact:

Truth:78 / Equipping the Next Generations
to Know, Honor, and Treasure God

Truth78.org

info@Truth78.org

877.400.1414

@Truth78org

THE AUTHORS

SALLY MICHAEL

Sally is a co-founder of Truth78 (originally called Children Desiring God) and has authored many resources for both children and adults, including 20 curricula, 10 books, and several booklets. For 16 years, Sally was also the Minister for Resources and Program Development at Bethlehem Baptist Church in Minneapolis, serving under the leadership of John Piper and David Michael. Her ministry has been marked by a passion for developing God-centered resources for the spiritual development of children. Sally and her husband, David, live in Indianapolis where they serve families at College Park Church. They enjoy spending time with their daughter Kristi, daughter Amy and her husband Gary, and three grandchildren.

JILL NELSON

Jill has taught Sunday school for more than 30 years. Her desire for God-centered, Gospel-focused, biblically rich teaching led her to write children's and youth curriculum for Truth78 (originally called Children Desiring God). Some titles include: *Jesus, What a Savior*, *The ABCs of God*, *To Be Like Jesus*, and *Your Word Is Truth*. She also develops training seminars, articles, and other resources relating to children's and youth ministry. She and her husband, Bruce, live in the Minneapolis area and enjoy spending time with their daughter Sarah and her husband Matt, son Jacob and his wife Amanda, and five grandchildren.